ASK THE COW
A GENTLE GUIDE TO FINDING PEACE

Rita M. Reynolds

PublishingWorks, Inc.

Exeter, NH

2008

PublishingWorks, Inc.,
60 Winter Street
Exeter, NH 03833
603-778-9883

For Sales and Orders:
1-800-738-6603 or 603-772-7200

Cover design by Kat Mack.
Cover photo copyright © by Michael Reynolds
Text design by Anna Godard.

LCCN: 2007937264
ISBN: 1-933002-58-1
ISBN-13: 978-1-933002-58-3

Printed In Canada

Ask the Cow

Dedicated to my grandmother
Elizabeth Williams Chandler
who taught me to believe and trust and to never give up.

Contents

ACKNOWLEDGMENTS

There are so many of you—wonderful friends and colleagues around the world who encourage and support all the work I do. You know who you are because you walk beside me in our shared spirit of reverence for all beings. We cheer one another on through the toughest of times, and celebrate together each step humanity makes toward a greater, more compassionate awareness. I wish I could name each and every one of you! Please know how grateful I am for knowing you.

I would like to especially thank my husband, Doug, my sons Michael and Tim, my "adopted daughter" Jo, my sister Sylvia, all for their complete faith in me, and Jeremy Townsend at PublishingWorks, who has enthusiastically embraced *Ask the Cow* from the beginning and brought it out into the world.

FOREWORD

WHEN I READ RITA REYNOLDS'S FIRST BOOK, BLESSING *the Bridge: What Animals Teach Us about Death, Dying, and Beyond*, I was in that state of grief all too familiar to animal lovers, yet all too easy to brush aside by those who've never known the peaceful love of an animal companion. My beagle Lauren had been gone for longer than I liked to admit when I first picked up Blessing the Bridge. Still feeling hollow and fragile, I began to read, and as I read, I began to change the way I looked at death. Filled with wisdom and a touch of mysticism, Rita's book provided me with moments of profound joy that helped me through my grief and led me to acceptance. In receiving such a gift from a book, I almost felt it too much to ask that it also be well written. But it was. So I waited for another book from this author to appear. And I waited. Finally, one did. In its simple profundity, *Ask the Cow: A Gentle Guide to Peace* gave me goose bumps from the first chapter to the last.

Few writers are able to mix insight and wise philosophical perspective with humor, the comic view being infinitely harder to get right on paper than the tragic or dramatic. When done well, this combination is always compelling. Rita Reynolds is one such writer, who, by combining humility with hilarity, another worldly wisdom, together with a gentleness and simplicity that shines out from the pages of *Ask The Cow*, achieves a mastery that brings to mind Antoine de Saint Exupery or Michel de Montaigne.

But before I wax deliriously over Mrs. Reynolds, let's give credit where it's due: Christina the cow, Rita's teacher and muse, is the real heroine of this book. In an allegorical and metaphorical style, Rita records Christina's teachings, which illuminate the natural and mystical, speaking universal truths so plainly and casually, it's as if the keys to the universe were something everyone mastered in first grade; well, maybe only cows were able to do this. With understated humor and humble poise, *Ask the Cow* strips away the petty trivia of life that slows us down and stresses us out; it turns the profound simple, and makes me wonder how I never saw this before. In straightforward, easy-to-read chapters, *Ask the Cow* offers golden nuggets full of life's lessons, and a few secrets along the way—the kind that, after laughing out loud, make me say, "Wow!"

Now, having met this sage of a cow on numerous visits after I was lucky enough to have been introduced to her caretaker, I do attest that she is indeed an exceptional cow—even if she has not yet shared her philosophy with me. But don't doubt her, for if beauty is in the eye of the beholder, perhaps respectively, knowledge, or the ability to receive simple truths, is in the eye of the willing and daring. Witness Wilbur the pig; to many, he was no more than the early stages of sausage. To a passerby, Christina, Her Holy Cowship, may appear an unlikely sage, but to those souls who have once felt the pain of watching a human crush a spider, or who perhaps feel just the slightest urge to sit a few minutes as a cow chews her cud, an experience awaits that will leave you breathless from transcendence, and somehow purified.

Ask the Cow offers great insight, wisdom, and a sense of "knowing." It gives me joy and, most of all, peace. Ask the Cow teaches us to become still, to look to the obvious, which is the art of looking into our hearts. It teaches us to revere nature. If Pascal wrote of God, *Ask the Cow* speaks of grace. Who knows—maybe one day I'll achieve that state of grace if Christina offers to share one of her secrets with me. Until then, I'll keep reading and rereading this special book.

This book is for those who seek peace and insightfulness in their lives—for those who have felt the magic of an animal's guidance. This book is for those who know that truth lies not in tangible facts, but in our own hearts, and that courage is found when one follows the heart's call. This book is also for lovers of animals and seekers of truth everywhere.

—Kay Pfaltz, author of *Lauren's Story:*
An American Dog in Paris

Author's Non-disclaimer

It would be highly impractical to make the usually required statement: *The opinions expressed in this book are those of the cow and not the author,* because this simply is not the case. While many of the situations in which I found my beloved bovine are, indeed, fanciful, they are merely creative settings for the inspiration and wisdom I have received from her, all of which is absolutely true. Glenda Green writes in her book *Love Without End,* "Truth always transcends any story that presents it—be it real or fiction. Actually, many of the greatest truths and philosophical premises of all time have been advanced into consciousness through fictional or imaginative presentation." What is important is to know in your own heart if what is presented here is meaningful and helpful to you. Christina and I both hope that you find what you need here to guide your own journey. We wish you many blessings for the way.

Rita M. Reynolds
Batesville, Virginia

PROLOGUE

MEDITATIONS ON A TRASH CAN

CHRISTINA WALKED WITH PURPOSE IN HER EYES TO THE MIDDLE OF THE field, stopping in front of a battered, yet sturdy, blue plastic trash can. Dried mud around its exterior gave the can a "dressed-down" look, and a small vertical break along the rim showed it was a warrior who had seen tough times, much like a cat with a notch in his ear. Gently, Christina pressed the full length of her face against the can, tipping it slightly away from her so that she was balancing it on its bottom edge. And then she closed her eyes. For twelve minutes Christina remained in this position: head pressed, eyes closed, ever so slightly rocking the can back and forth on its edge without knocking it over.

"I've never seen a cow do *that* before," a visiting friend whispered to me. "What's she doing?"

"Meditating," I replied nonchalantly, as if this were a normal practice of hers. In fact, it was—and is—a daily ritual that Christina has performed each and every day of the past nine years she's lived here.

"I wonder if other cows do—that," my friend queried, obviously not convinced that a cow would meditate, and certainly not on such an object. She mentioned again that of all the cows she had seen, none had shared this habit.

"Given a trash can, they well might," I said thoughtfully, realizing that few farmers regarded their cattle as anything but commodities raised for monetary profit. Offering their cows meditation tools was probably not on their agricultural agenda.

Truth was, neither had it been on *my* mind in the early days of our bovine-human relationship. A resourceful youngster, Christina had

13

adopted me before I had a chance to clean the area of such objects as cast-off plastic trash cans. So she adopted the can as well, immediately showing her delight by sticking her head fully into it and raising it into the air until it rested upside down on her shoulders. Seeking the can as her primary meditation tool came later, as she matured and her impish-calf impulses began to surrender to deeper universal calls within her.

IT WAS JANUARY OF MY FORTY-NINTH YEAR WHEN CHRISTINA (as I soon named her), then a six-month-old russet-and-white Hereford calf, jogged up my driveway, fully expecting me to adopt her. I did, and we settled in to learn about one another, each growing in our own unique way.

In our first years together Christina focused on physical maturity, moving steadily upward and outward from a petite 250 pounds. I, however, turned my attention to finding my spiritual and emotional footing, slippery as it seemed to be at the time. As an animal caregiver for more than twenty-five years, I had come to work more and more with creatures who had disabilities, and those who were preparing for, and passing through, their dying. From each animal in my care I gained a clearer perspective, not only about death and dying, but also about living consciously—a clarity that only reinforced my innate respect and honor for all beings. Even now my current animal family included three donkeys, two goats, a dozen dogs (with many of them being old dogs), as many cats, ducks and chickens. I was delighted to add a cow to the crew.

Several years before Christina arrived at my door, I had even written a book about my experiences. I felt the knowledge and insight I had gained from the animals would be helpful to others who were dealing with the difficult loss of a companion animal. And I was right; following its initial publication in 2001, *Blessing the Bridge: What Animals Teach Us about Death, Dying, and Beyond*, would, indeed, help many people. Many people have written to thank me, saying they wished they had my strong spiritual sense of things. And certainly, at times I felt that I did have such a sense.

But in this temporal, physical world, very little remains the same for long. By the time this enchanting little calf strode into my barn, I was once again struggling hard with those endlessly persistent issues, such as mindfulness, patience forgiveness, frustration, fear, and anger. I *assumed* that all of these boiled down to the knowledge and application of inner and outer peace. I craved that kind of peace; I was anxious to find it in any way I could. So while Christina expanded with grace and delight, carrying her trash can around on her head or knocking it over the closest fence, I turned my attention back to a practice of study and meditation, and to consciously listening to my beloved, unseen—yet ever-present and reliable—spirit guides and guardians. But I found it to be a tough haul up a muddy slope, and I was fast losing ground.

One very warm midsummer day in 2003, I was feeling particularly drained, emotionally as well as physically. My human limitations were roaring, and my sense of inadequacy, persistent. Just to get fresh air and some distance from my concerns, I went out to the barn and sat down next to Christina, now a more-settled six years old, while she slept, snuggled down in her hay. As I leaned against her, I was surprised to find that I began to feel strong and sure of my direction in life again, able to deal with (well, nearly) anything. In those first moments of deeper connection between us, Christina became my anchor to peace, and that muddy slope leveled back out to become firm ground beneath my feet.

But when I left her presence to return to the seemingly infinite maze of responsibilities, the tough issues of my life closed back in around me. Sometimes when I would be feeding her or cleaning her stall, I would look into her eyes, and her unfaltering gaze would seem to say to me: *So, when are you going to ask for help?* I didn't, and she waited—patiently, as cows will do.

Then on a particularly stressful day (the kind where everything seems to go wrong from the moment you wake up), I went to my cow companion specifically to ask one question that wouldn't leave my already-overwrought brain. Her response to me—something I could clearly hear in my mind—stunned, delighted, and intrigued me. Her words felt completely appropriate and valid. I was hooked, and came back the next day to ask another question; from that moment on, I became her devoted student. What follows is an account of the journey Christina and I walked together that first full year—since I asked and she responded—leading me forward (as she contin-ues to do) through an ever more beautiful garden of spiritual awareness.

1   ASK THE COW

ACTUALLY, I WAS GETTING READY FOR MY WEEKLY SUPPLY RUN TO Charlottesville on a bright August morning when I thought of my first question for Christina. I had started out the morning with a wearily familiar complaint: *My life is always out of control.* Not really expecting that a solution was possible to such a dilemma, I paid no attention to the question and hurried through my morning chores. Then I dropped the car keys in my rush to get out the back door—in order to rush through the shopping so that I could rush home, and be in time to rush through afternoon and evening animal feeding and throw together my human family's dinner. If tradition held true, I would be late with everything, right on down the line.

As I ran down the walkway to the garden gate, I saw Christina watching me from her post-breakfast place in the barn. Cud spun around her jaws; she never rushed around. So, why did I? And then that stubborn question loomed larger and louder in my brain. Even so, I looked at my watch, and, feeling obligated to get on with my schedule, opened the car door. What actually made me then close the door and climb over Christina's fence, away from the car and the impending whirlwind of errands, I really can't say. But the pull was magnetic, and my desire for answers, suddenly powerful. I walked across the small stretch of packed bluestone in front of the barn and looked directly into her unblinking eyes.

"Christina," I said, "where is inner peace, and how do I find it?" I sat down next to her in the warm, crisp hay and waited patiently for her reply. It might well be a long time coming, considering the distant look on her face. Her massive head swung sedately toward me, her jaws never missing a beat.

"Cud," she said, her thought penetrating my mind in a voice that reverberated with the essence of the spoken word. With measured ease, the well-chewed wad of grass slipped down her throat, pausing in whichever of the four stomach chambers it was meant for, then—*zip!* Up it returned for a third round on her molars. "Start there."

"Please elaborate," I said, my curiosity stirred. But Christina's reply was only silence as she once again turned her head forward and, with neck ever so slightly extended, eyes half-closed, she drifted off to realms meant only for cows. Our session was apparently over.

I decided to stay home for the rest of the day, and during the remainder of the afternoon I pondered on her single answer. My head buzzed with questions and ideas, all spilling out over one another. Why such brevity? Did she mean cud itself, and if so, in its totality, or broken down into its separate elements? Was she referring to the process of chewing, swallowing, and/or regurgitation? And how did any of this relate to obtaining inner peace?

Obviously, another session with Christina was called for, and without the formality of making an appointment, I simply showed up at her stall the next morning, even though the errands of the day before were still not done. But having coexisted with Her Cowship for six years, I was keenly aware of her precise habits and strict schedule. Only at certain hours would she be available for in-depth discourse. For example, breakfast and dinner times were definitely out of the question. Her attention would be focused on Matters of Great Importance. Grazing times, likewise, would be off limits, only because her nose would be pointed downward, making essential eye contact limited or impossible. And trying to gather her wisdom delivered through a mouthful of grass? *Rft mrnng f lhjfle ss wlufnl...*

It was 9:28 in the morning on this particular summer's day, exceptionally hot already, with everything in nature sweating like a human. And so was I. Nonetheless, I felt that pursuit of higher learning displaced personal comfort, and so, settled next to an equally sweat-drenched beast of ever-expanding physical and spiritual dimensions, I once again queried my bovine companion.

"Christina," I began optimistically, heading straight to my point, "I am confused. Please help. Regarding cud and achieving inner peace..." Upon my calling her name, her head began its downward, sideways trip to study me with those enormous dark and luminous eyes. Her current bunch of grass and hay rested comfortably in her square jaws.

"Brevity—and attention to detail," she began. "Keep it simple. Life and everything about it. Chew your ideas with care, swallow your pride, be willing to cough up when necessary." The grass disappeared down her throat. "Does that help?" Her eyes remained buttoned to mine.

"Yes, but..." I said weakly, trying to ingest her words.

"Waste nothing," she continued, never losing eye contact in a somewhat unnerving manner. "Love everything you do, even—*especially*—the mundane things. And above all, remember: Keep it simple; give it back."

"Give *what* back?" I begged. But once again the session appeared to be over, signaled, as always, by the return of face-to-forward, slight extension of neck, drifty half-stare of the eyes: one cow gone again to other realms meant only or.... Perhaps tomorrow—so much to consider. How could something as vital as inner peace be so confusing and elusive? I thanked her, of course, and rubbed her chin, a favorite way of paying my respect to my friend.

From the onset of our relationship, Christina had proven to be not only my special friend, but also, far more than what I had once erroneously believed to be just another cow. In fact, from the moment that wisp of a calf appeared in my driveway, she not only moved herself right onto the homestead, but she also established a firm footing in my heart. Without a group of her own, she apparently viewed me as her herd, and herself, the herd leader, a sure sign of things to come. I was immediately entranced by her.

Still, I felt legally bound to locate her "owner" (not a word I would choose), and soon learned that he was renting the land behind us and she was, indeed, the only—and very lonely—cow there. No wonder she had come searching for a family. But the man seemed to want her back. The next day, after much rushing about, waving of arms, begging and shouting, together with the man's brother-in-law, we coaxed her back through the fence dividing our properties. I boldly informed the man that he could never sell or eat this calf, for I had fallen in love with her. Although he was amused by my declaration, he was unimpressed.

It would seem that Christina had been paying attention, however, for three hours later, she returned, having once again broken out far up in the back field and trudged down two roads to stand, rather disgruntled, at the bottom of our driveway. Determination was set in her jaw; her eyes flashed fire: "*Must* we keep doing this?" I could feel her say.

Once again I phoned the farmer, but he was tired of his

errant calf and unwilling to mend his fence on such a cold January day. And so, he sold her to me for $65, the exact amount of money (unbeknownst to him) that I had recently received as a Christmas gift—a bargain without question.

Now I faced the question of what to do with this beast in the middle of winter, ice storm pending, not to mention that this was my first experience with the bovine set. I learned quickly, though, and as she grew, so did my knowledge of the basic what's and what-not's of cattle care giving. And we did well, learning about one another, except for the time she got her head stuck under the board fence trying to reach for a blade of grass, and another time when she lifted the metal gate off its hinges and escaped to munch the delicacies of my flower garden.

Smart as a cat, early on she learned how to whip the dogs into a frenzy (they share a common fence line) by rushing about, tucking into one of her two stalls, and then disappearing from their view. As dogs will do, they charged up and down the fence trying to find her, only to sit in confusion and despair when they failed to do so. Just then Christina would poke her nose around the corner of her house as if to say, "Yoo-hoo, here I am!"—and they were off once again. Harriet, my keen friend and next-door neighbor, was quick to appreciate Christina's intelligence. While discussing an incident in which "my" cow showed obvious prowess, Harriet listened, studying Christina thoughtfully. Then she remarked, "Ah yes, much more than a pretty face."

Even before my search for inner peace, Christina was determined to offer me introductory lessons on honoring the inner child—or inner calf, depending on one's viewpoint. "Oh boy!" she would exclaim with unbounded joy, leaping sideways like a grasshopper without inhibition each time I arrived at the back gate with her feed bucket. *Play*, Christina tells me still, *is uncharted territory, wide open to all combinations and possibilities.* She demonstrated this particular lesson by charging the plastic trash can, at that time her favorite toy. Obediently, the can would roll over, surrendering to the moment. Perhaps to clarify her point for me, she then squashed it against one of her water buckets, thus tipping the bucket over and creating a delicious mudslide upon which she seemed determined to try and break at least one leg.

"Now," my beauteous beast would then proclaim, directly facing me, "pay attention, because..." But each time I failed to hear the rest, for I was skimming the fence as her lowered head made for my knees. Perhaps in her eyes there was no difference between a trash can and myself, possibly an early lesson in humility, a first unconscious step toward inner peace?

Nine twenty-eight on a Thursday morning, August 7, in a stall looking out over Virginia's magnificent Blue Ridge Mountains: one desperate human, searching; a placid Hereford heifer; and the usual swarm of flies. I felt I had to ask: "Regarding your statement, 'Give it back,' " I began hopefully.

The massive face turned, eyes rolled to meet mine, and jaws paused in mid-swing. Cud quivered down her throat.

"We don't own it," she stated.

"Own *what?*" I squealed.

"Anything. Everything."

"I don't want to own *everything*," I wailed pitifully. "I just want inner peace, and I don't see what chewing cud has to do with it."

"I didn't say that cud is the only way to achieve inner peace," Christina said, maintaining that bovine composure. "It's a step, but not the most important one." Her head started its forward trek; eyelids began to droop. I scooted around to face her. Her eyes widened as her head drew back.

"Wait a minute here," I said, "*You* just said..."

She looked patiently at me, then sighed. "Start where you are, with who you are. Be very quiet and listen to what your heart tells you: What do you love to do? What do you believe in? Who do you love—animals, trees, people, water? And keep following your feeling here. Do they make you feel wonderful? What do you see yourself giving back to the world, the Earth, to others? All of these are *your own truth*, your unbounded Self, the essence that is embodied in your physical form, but is neither limited to, nor dictated by, that form. And once you really pay attention to all that already lives in your heart and start living those things, then *bingo!* You will realize *you* are and always have been, peace through and through—inner, outer, everywhere, everything, no boundaries, no doubts, no limitations, no fears, no frustrations."

I must have looked confused. And I was; my brain was still struggling to equate all of this with the chewing and processing of wads of grass. Christina paused and looked at me thoughtfully.

"Hmmm. Think of it this way, then," she said kindly. "The easiest way to understand and live the truth that lives in your heart is to accept, enjoy, nourish, and then return with gratitude to others, the goodness that is always available to you. Take only what you need, use it wisely and respectfully, give back generously, and always say *thank you*. Or, in a word: cud."

She closed her eyes; it seemed that our interview was over. But then a hearty belch and a comfortable sigh preceded her final words: "And always honor your inner calf." With her neck extended just so, her eyelids half-closed, Christina drifted off effortlessly to those realms meant only for cows.

I still had so many questions! Find my truth? A big order for a short person, but I was willing to try. Patience with my cow-turned-wise-teacher seemed an appropriate first step. And so, trusting that our lessons would continue another day (at her discretion, of course), I pulled my car keys from my pocket and strode off to my car, boldly saying, "Yes! I can do this!" And I didn't feel rushed at all.

2   JUNK DRAWER

THE NEXT DAY I WAS IN A VERY GOOD MOOD. THE MORNING WAS FINE–SUNNY, warm–and no one in my animal sanctuary was sick, let alone dying, a remarkable and unusual day around here. But the meringue on *this* "pie" was that I was feeling very pleased with myself. Yesterday's trip to Char lottesville for supplies had gone smoothly, and I was actually home ahead of schedule. But more than anything, I was enthusiastic about my initial session with Christina. Inner peace was nearly mine.

Now it was time for a break from my day's routine. I ambled out into the sunlight, singing "What a Day for a Daydream," an old favorite from my college days. I was so caught up in the highs and lows of the lyrics that I nearly bumped into my blessed cow. She was bent over some‑thing invisible, shuffling her left front hoof back and forth, three or four inches off the ground. My good mood and curiosity teamed up with a cheery, "Whatcha doing, young lady?"

Considerable grunting ensued, words I could not distinguish mumbled as if deep within something cavernous. I wondered how she did that when nothing cavernous was evident. A bovine sneeze followed, by another sneeze, followed by another, followed by...

"Bless you!" I offered politely. "Cold coming on?"

"Dust," she replied, barely lifting her head. But the soil was moist from a recent rain; no dust was evident. None of those facts seemed to matter in Christina's personal reality, a reality unlike any other known to humans, as I would soon learn during our subsequent lessons together.

Christina lifted her massive, broad head and furrowed her brow. Well, she tried to, anyway, and I got the point.

"It's just not in there," she sighed, taking her foot and shoving the invisible something away from her.

"Should I ask?" I said casually. She turned her large, very deep eyes toward me and looked with what I defensively read as sorrow for the ignorant human standing before her.

"Don't slump," she said sternly.

Instinctively I straightened my back, but stuck my hands in the pockets of my jeans to present a casual yet defiant facade to my rather overbearing teacher. She only nodded approvingly, then turned back to her task at, er, hoof.

"What are you looking for?" I asked innocently.

She appeared to be rummaging again. "I'm looking for the spare screwdriver I keep in here so that I can fix my confusion. Both of them should be in here someplace."

Questions, so many questions. I thought I'd just dive in with: "Screwdriver?"

"Yes," she replied from the depths of the invisible something. "You haven't seen it, have you? It's one of those Fat Max ones, the really good kind with the padded handle—"

"Confusion?" I interrupted, in my usual one-track fashion.

"—can be both a flathead and a Phillips screwdriver with just a twist of—"

"Here? Where is *here?*" I felt like I was losing consciousness, or else the world was beginning to swirl, or...

"—a little button on the end so you can use it in all kinds of situations."

I just stared at her now. I was out of questions.

"It was here just the other day when I had to fix my insecurity. Darn." Finally my silence attracted her attention.

"What were you saying?" she asked, coming up for a breath of dust-free air. "Oh," she said. "Don't you have one of these in *your* kitchen?"

"One of what?" I ventured cautiously.

"A junk drawer! You know, a kitchen drawer where you can dump rubber bands that come around broccoli stalks, toothpicks, the can opener, that spare screw driver, measuring spoons, insecurities, fears, anger, sorrow...*What?*"

I had raised my hands in a customary gesture of surrender.

"In *my* kitchen junk drawer," I said, "yes, I have rubber bands, a screwdriver, pliers, scissors, two thousand twist ties, bottle caps to who knows what, and old, half-burned birthday candles. *And that is all*, except, of course, for the can opener and box of stick matches. THAT is a normal junk drawer. Besides, I thought you were so enlightened you never got confused or insecure." I could feel my face heating up and inner peace slipping to the left.

"And," I continued, "I do not see any drawer in front of you, or a kitchen. *What are you keeping in that drawer again?*"

Christina looked patiently at me, letting those miraculous long white lashes drop slowly across her eyes, then raise up like angel's wings, revealing eyes ablaze with humor and love.

"My drawer," she said, "is visible only to me because it *pertains* to me, in my 'kitchen' where I 'cook up' my reality moment by moment. You see, I am as subject to the whims and follies of earthly illusion as humans are, and I lose track of my way in life—or, to say it another way, my *truth*. You know how it is: 'Stuff happens,' and when it does, one's truth tends to get buried in the pile. So I have my junk drawer where I can place all my 'stuff' that troubles me, and then find a tool in that same drawer to correct it so that I can reconnect with my truth. After all, when we get to lesson 451B, you will learn that all problems contain their own solutions. Perhaps a quick preview course is needed?"

I shook my head, but I was hardly paying attention; I was still deeply embedded in my need to physically *see* a drawer. Then the Queen of Cows raised her chin just so, and at four inches above the ground, a small, neatly formed wooden drawer appeared. There was no kitchen, no other cabinetry, just the drawer. I wished for more. She shook her head.

"This is enough," she stated quietly. "May I recommend that you create your own personal *other* junk drawer, for all the negative, unwanted, uncomfortable thoughts and ideas that take you away from what is truthful and meaningful for you. But be sure and add the necessary tools to correct those thoughts and ideas." She was pensive for a moment. "For example," she said, shifting her bulk to a more comfortable position, "in my drawer I have among my tools a pair of three-D glasses.

Do you remember those? Made from paper with lenses out of cellophane, one green, one red?"

"What would you use those for?" I asked.

"For seeing past illusion to the truth of the matter. Puts everything in a different perspective. Very handy in a crisis."

I peered inside her drawer and saw nothing.

"Of course," she said softly, "this is *my* drawer, and it fits my agenda. If I were to look into your personal junk drawer—not your house-kitchen one, of course—I, too, would see nothing. You cannot see what is relevant only to my own experience, and vice versa. It's a good plan, I promise you. I also keep a flashlight in here," she said, "to help me find my way (figuratively speaking, of course). And when someone speaks hurtfully to me, or I am feeling badly about myself, though you can't see them, I do have a box of birthday candles in here—not half-burned, either—to remind me that I am, each moment, worth celebrating."

She took that left front hoof and gently "closed" the drawer so that it disappeared into another dimension beyond my vision. "Rubber bands," she said pensively, "are for when I feel scattered, too many things to do in too little time, and an old key to goodness knows where, to remind me to look to the Great Mystery for the answers to all my questions. The 'key' opens many doors on many levels, seen and unseen, and keeps the adventure of life and beyond always exciting and inspiring. Good to keep a spare key for that as well. Oh, and a set of measuring spoons. Yes, here they are!"

"Why measuring spoons?" I asked.

"Sometimes even I forget to be focused about something. The idea of precise measurement helps me to remember."

She seemed to once again be lost in thought when suddenly, she shifted her gaze to the right. "And, my favorite," she sighed. "A spare coffee scoop." She looked at me, waiting for my response, but I was stumped.

"Comfort food!" she exclaimed happily. "Never forget the comfort food." She seemed to be rooting around in the drawer for something else. "Ah, here it is!" she cried, reaching one foot forward to grasp something invisible in midair. "The screwdriver!" she exclaimed with delight. "I knew it was in here somewhere. Now, where did I put that confusion of mine?"

I wished her well in her endeavors and started back toward the house. There were just too many questions jamming my brain, all those issues I thought I had stored under SOLVED in order to leave room for those highly desirable treasures called truth and peace. But if my spiritually advanced cow-teacher needed comfort food, not to mention focus in her life, what hope was there for me?

I decided to keep busy doing something useful, and it occurred to me that I could clean my kitchen junk drawer. If nothing else, I knew I had a spare coffee scoop...

3   A SERIOUS CASE
OF THOREAU

AND THAT DRAWER WAS ONE HORRIFYING MESS. IN FACT, I HAD to tug and pry and say some powerful words before I could even budge it. *What a metaphor for my life,* I thought sadly, suddenly feeling overwhelmed. But I was determined to clean out and organize the drawer and what its contents represented. *After all,* I muttered as I kept yanking on its wrought-iron handle, *this is my drawer and my life; no one else is responsible for either one, except me.* Then, with one foot braced against the bottom cabinet, teeth clenched, and both hands pulling as hard as possible, I wrenched the overstuffed drawer loose, sending us both—along with a thousand twist ties, pliers, old candles, and whatever else—backward on to the kitchen floor.

Previous to my first session with Christina, I would have immediately abandoned the task of untangling the "stuff" that now lay on top of and all around me, made a pot of coffee, and called it a day. I realized one of four options stood before me: One, push it all back in the drawer and return the drawer to its "cubby" in the cabinet. Two, throw everything away and duct-tape the drawer back together, since it now seemed to have a few less necessary parts (also all over the floor). Three, push all the contents into a bag for sorting through on one of those famous "other days." But, in light of Christina's wise words about sorting out one's inner truth, the fourth and final option seemed the only way to go, a task I then began, but not without a heavy sigh. Placing the now-empty drawer aside to be repaired later, I began organizing the scattered contents into piles, while the hard floor beneath me hinted that my search for inner peace was not going to necessarily be an easy job.

But then I came upon a small box of animal candle holders:

tiny giraffes, a brightly painted pony, a pleasant faced, golden lion, and two wooden birds, one pink, the other blue. At the bottom of the box was The Old Goat, a red plastic toy that we've always added to every birthday cake as a joke. These little creatures had graced cakes throughout my two sons' childhoods, and now, for me, they ignited happy memories of family gatherings and the deep affection we hold for one another. For several minutes I sat on the floor, tenderly holding the tiny animals in my hands as if they were the greatest treasure in the world. And indeed, in my heart, they were. Everything around me, including the floor, felt warm and soft.

I remembered something Christina had recently said to me. We had been talking about looking objectively at what was really important to me—my own belief system, as it were; what connected me to others—people, animals, trees, ideas, visions and dreams—even including whatever task I chose to undertake. "That connection is like a reciprocal, unwritten companionship between you and *All* That Is," Christina had said. "When you can absolutely feel that connection in your heart, everything makes sense and becomes easy because the energy between you will flow."

Because this was a difficult concept for me to understand, she elaborated: "For example, water intuitively knows its truth or purpose: to cycle through the atmosphere, back to Earth as rain, collect in streams and rivers, and eventually return to the oceans to cycle back up into the atmosphere once again. And there is no struggle in any of this process because water is simply doing what it knows it is meant to do, and it does so willingly."

I must have mentally questioned water having the ability to understand its purpose, because Christina then replied, "Everything has life and the ability to understand its purpose. And so do you."

Sitting on that kitchen floor, I realized that the best place to begin to *willingly* understand my purpose—my truth—was by attacking the piles from my jumbled, over-full junk drawer, now waiting all around me for my attention. And I was making excellent progress when the phone rang; it was a friend, asking if I could find a home for two adult cats who were about to be euthanized. The cats needed to be re-homed together, as they were siblings and very attached to one another. I thought of their person who had apparently died suddenly, leaving them orphaned. I knew that in her spirit-self, she would be very concerned about her cats.

I reached to turn on my computer in order to start contacting possible homes, but the Internet connection would not stay on. I picked up the phone to make calls instead, and found the line was dead. Frustration began to seep into my willingness. Time to visit Christina again for some good bovine inspiration.

"Know what?" I said, as I stepped into the feed shed to get Christina's supper.

"If you say so," she replied, obviously neither paying attention to my question, nor interested in my line of thought. The bovine brain was focused solely on my hand opening the grain bin. She poked her head through the door behind me and tried to press the rest of her ampleness inside. But too much interest in previous meals made her now look like Winnie-the-Pooh stuck in Rabbit's doorway. I had a captive audience.

"Know what?" I repeated.

Impatience furrowed her brow. You know the type—loves to pontificate when it suits her, but lapses into long, personal silences at the most unexpected moments.

"Give me a shove, will you?" she grumbled.

"Know what?" I said yet again. This time, there was a bit of a wicked smirk tucked into the corners of my mouth. For such a stolid, centered beast, my cow was losing it. Figuratively, of course.

"WHAT??" she shouted back at me, totally out of character. And when a cow (who eats garlic twice a day) shouts, the effect is noteworthy. Pulling myself off the back wall, I once again approached my beloved. Her four empty stomachs were calling loudly; her eyes blazed. With all the effort I had, I pushed and shoved, but her massive body wouldn't budge. I sat down on one of the feed bins to assess the situation. *What was I thinking?* A paltry human trying to dislodge a very stuck, quite over-weight, and—*what?* While I had been trying to shove the dear thing out of the shed door, Christina, obviously forgetting the project at hand, had refocused on the feed can and was trying to push her way back in.

"As I was trying to say," I sighed, "this is so typical of my life. No matter what my intentions are to find order and peace, I end up with chaos." There was the very real possibility we could remain in such a fix for a very long time. More likely was the chance that, so driven by the need to reach the grain, Christina might actually disassemble the door and walls, bringing the roof down on top of us. Not a pleasant thought, especially since I was still sore from my earlier forceful encounter with the kitchen floor. I looked her straight in the eye. "On the count of three," I said firmly, "stop thinking about food and step backwards. Then you get to eat! One, two—"

There was a frightening crack and groan to the door frame, but before I could reach *three*, she plowed backward with such force that she shot across to the fence and bounced—once. I was impressed. Feed can still in hand, I proceeded across the grass to her food dish. Embarrassed, Christina shuffled behind me and without further comment, shoveled her broad pink nose into her hard-won dinner. I sat down on the ground beside her, absorbing the soothing sounds of grinding, chewing, and swallowing. *All right, she wasn't going to listen to me, but I was going to speak my thoughts anyway.* I had come out to the barn needing counsel and I intended to fulfill my goal.

"Know what? *Here's* what," I said, looking around for a suitable victim. A ladybug—one of the four thousand sharing home and yard, made the unfortunate (for her) choice of landing on my hand. "The sad truth still remains that there's too much going on in my life," I said directly to the ladybug. I hoped I had her attention, even though she turned away from me. "Every moment is filled: too many responsibilities and obligations; too many machines that break down; too much running from here to there and back to here again; and everybody wants something from me. How can I ever find the time to find inner peace, let alone discover what I'm supposed to be doing with my life?"

The ladybug yawned.

"So, am I boring you?" I asked sarcastically. My mood had darkened.

"She can't understand you," said a voice behind me, muffled by the remnants of corn, oats, and molasses. I turned around to see Christina calmly gathering the last crumbs of grain from her dish. "She can't understand you," my cow continued, "because you're sending out too much negative energy and disrupting a ladybug's naturally peaceful aura. In a word or three: She can't relate."

"But *you* can hear me," I replied.

"I have broader shoulders."

I studied her from several angles but couldn't find any shoulders at all.

"I was speaking symbolically," she said, reading my thoughts.

The ladybug had disappeared, but I seemed to have Christina's attention, so I tried one more time. "Know what?" I asked, limply this time.

Christina perked up. "Yes! I know everything: what, where, why, to

32

whom... and the weather for next Thursday. Any more questions?"

"That's not funny," I continued. "There's no room in my day anymore for many of activities I love."

"Such as?"

"Reading. Sitting under the maple tree in the front yard. Listening to the birds sing at dawn. Being still. *Inner peace*, for goodness' sake."

"Relating to ladybugs on a positive level," Christina added, trying to be helpful.

I frowned at her and plunged back into my own misery. "I'm serious," I said. "I want—my *soul* needs—time and opportunity to reenter the natural world around me and to hear deep, inspiring thoughts... but I don't know how to go about it."

Christina burped politely, folded her front legs beneath her, and sank to the soft nest of hay she had made for herself. "Oh, you shouldn't worry," she said calmly. "You're just experiencing a serious case of Thoreau."

"A case of *what?*" I asked belligerently.

"Thoreau," she replied patiently. "You've heard of him, haven't you? Henry David, the philosopher who occasionally dabbled in writing. He, too, got fed up with all the people and things and silly chatter. He fled to Walden Pond; called it an experiment in living. A cop-out is what it really was, even though it was ultimately a good decision. You should read the book."

I stared at her. Words wouldn't come. Well, words stuck, then peeled themselves apart, marched directly over to her, and tapped her on her existential shoulders. "How do you know about Henry David Thoreau?" I asked. "And I have read the book!"

"Henry?" she replied calmly. "We go back a long way. Buddies in the war and all that. Spent some time at Walden with him, actually, when I was one of the town mice. I went everywhere with him— in his pocket, mind you. Truth is, *Walden*, chapter twelve, 'Brute Neighbors'—I wrote that one."

"You did not!"

"Sure did. You see, Henry was pretty good with budgets and building cabins, but he didn't really understand animals very well; he needed my help in relating to them." Christina's eyes blurred, a sign she was deep in recall. "That was one of my finest pieces of writing," she said. "Of course, Henry had a hand in it. I didn't want to steal his writing style, you know. Yes, Henry got fed up with the town life one night. We were sharing some supper, and Henry started going on just like you were a minute ago. In fact, I believe he started with something like, 'Know what?'"

"You're laughing at me," I said.

"Not at all, "Christina replied. "He felt the same as you, so naturally he expressed it the same way you just did. Makes sense to me. But he *acted* on his distress: got up from supper and moved to Walden Pond." She gave me that look. "So, what are you going to do about *your* case of Thoreau?"

"I think I'll go and eat something," I said weakly. "Chocolate." I got up off the ground and started for the house, but turned back to add, "I suppose Thoreau ate chocolate, too?"

"Absolutely. Who do you think introduced him to comfort food?" Christina shifted from foot to foot to foot to foot. That meant, *You didn't answer my question.*

"Okay," I sighed. "I guess I'll try and find time to—"

My sweet teacher broke in firmly: "Go—right now—sit under the maple tree, listen to the birds. All the busyness and machines and noise you feel so trapped by will simply flow around you for a while, just as water flows around a large rock in a stream. You are the rock! And for those moments, you, too, will become strong, silent, and serene, and find the peace you're looking for. But first you have to decide to do it. Now, go and let it be easy."

"Okay," I said. "I'll do it—but it will have to wait until I find two sad cats a new home..."

Christina hit me with her most piercing look. "Want to choose something different here?" she asked flatly.

I thought about the cats; having to call the phone company to report the outage; struggling with an inadequate Internet server; the blessed kitchen drawer... I straightened my shoulders. "You know what, Christina? I think I'll just go sit under that maple tree for a while."

"Ah, yes... Henry would be so pleased," Christina said, closing her eyes, perhaps to listen to the birds singing their afternoon songs.

At that precise moment, the ladybug flew down to my hand. "Hello again," I said pleasantly as I walked around to the front of the house. She turned and looked up at me, for this time, she had heard me. "Let me tell you about these two really fine cats..."

4   LAVENDER EARTHWORMS

AND GUESS WHAT? THOSE TWO FINE, HOMELESS CATS, DUSTY and Sweetpea, came to live with *me.* Thanks to that one ladybug, I had begun paying closer attention to my own intuition—those feelings and desires that Christina referred to as My Truth, sitting deeply in my gut. And my gut clearly said to me, *Those cats belong here.* Okay, I would trust my intuition; a good opportunity to test myself, because I knew what a responsibility I would be taking on—not just one cat, but two. I wasn't disappointed. Dusty and Sweetpea turned out to be wonderful creatures: gentle, peaceful, playful, and loving, excellent new members of my animal family.

Encouraged, I found that it was becoming easier to follow my instincts and Christina's advice, especially when I took more time to just sit and lean against a favorite tree, watch spiders spin their webs, or contemplate the fluidity of clouds, all unending miracles for me. The more I stayed clear and focused in the present moment, aware of the environment around me, the more miracles revealed themselves to me. So I shouldn't have been so surprised when my cow presented me with a new view of reality.

"Do people come in purple, too?" Christina suddenly asked me between bites of sweet feed one morning around ten o'clock. Considering she had been silent most of the day, her unexpected yet casually posed question disoriented me. I must have focused on the wrong part of her question when I rebounded with: "*Too?*"

She eyed me with uncertainty; confusion edged her voice: "Also?"

"Excuse me?" I replied, now completely lost.

"I said," she replied, "should I have used the word 'also' instead of the word 'too'?" Her head dipped slightly in a motion of embarrassment. Among many fine qualities, Christina is a cow with a fairly decent handle on grammatical usage. Not I, however. Never one for details, proper grammar continually eludes me. And so I had to honestly reply: "I don't know what word you should have used, nor do I understand why you used it." I was becoming agitated.

"No need to get all bothered-up," she said, returning to the project at hand, being breakfast. "I was only curious as to whether your species—"

"Yes, yes, something about being purple?"

"*If* you would kindly let me finish... ," Christina said as she turned toward her stall and burped.

Great, I thought. *This means she's heading in for her nap and I still have no idea what she was talking about.* No need to fight it. Napping, in Christina's opinion, is always sacred time, and interruptions are not allowed. Suppressing my frustration, I finished my chores and started toward the house.

"I only thought..." came wafting across the air currents behind me, and I turned to see my massive bovine companion looking mournfully in my direction. Dejection rocked her aura. I walked back to her and wrapped my arms around her neck.

"Now, what about people being purple?" I asked.

"Too," she added.

"Yes, too, but too what? Or whom? And what are we talking about?"

"Well," she began, beckoning me into her stall, "recently I have been contemplating the personality of things, and it occurred to me that each being has its own dominant tone, sound, and color. You, being born in mid-April and thus an Aries, are definitely an E major and a brilliant but not flashy yellow, like the sun. I, on the other hoof, am a C minor and a deep purple-blue, like that of a Japanese iris. You may be interested to know that most cows tend toward the purple hues. I was just wondering if some people did as well. That was all." She settled into her bed of fresh hay and sighed happily. Philosophical wonderment ranks high on her list of hobbies.

I thought of all the cows and humans I had encountered throughout my fifty-some years and was unable to remember a one who struck me as being a purple. Except my mother. Christina read my thoughts. "Ah yes, a wise and kindly person, your mama. So mystical, even when she was in-body. Oh yes, definitely a purple lady. Thank you; you have answered my question." And she turned away as if our conversation was done.

"But you only met my mother once," I challenged.

"Oh, no—we are most excellent friends!" Christina arched her head back and forth to indicate infinity. "Your mama's spirit is—"

"Is what?" I asked anxiously, interrupting again. Somehow we had gone from discussing color to the location of my mother's soul, and I sure did miss my mother. Christina looked down at me with incredible patience, which I may (or may not) have deserved. When she next spoke, she did so kindly. "Your mother's spirit is often here."

"And is she still a purple?" I asked, trying to get back to the original subject. There were too many loose ends there to be drifting off into talk of spirits and souls.

Christina sighed happily. "Most definitely. Funny how I never saw that before."

"So if Mom's a purple, and you're a purple, does that mean my mother's soul and my cow are—"

"It means that our personalities are attuned to one another," Christina said, picking at her foot as if everything was normal on the farm. After all, one's parents move on and cows graze. But with Christina on board things have a way of flip-flopping in a most remarkable manner. She was studying me again. Those enormous brown eyes pierced my consciousness and drew me back into two realizations. One was that I was mentally babbling and she was waiting for me to stop. The other was that I was sitting in the presence of a very grand (and not just speaking of the poundage) and wise being. Suddenly, purple seemed to fit her well.

"Thank you," she said with true humility, reading my mind once again.

"Now frogs," she continued with determination, "are more often of the bluer tints, while you might be interested to know that most rabbits are of a pinker nature. It's their innate timidity and innocence, you understand." Her broad face stared at me, expecting my full attention. And she had it. I began to wonder about other creatures. Worms, for instance.

"Worms?" she replied, again catching my thought. "Your standard earthworms are lavender. But your night crawlers are, oh! Such a magnificent ruby red. Reflects their exceptionally loving nature. Did you know that?" I shook my head, but she was sighing wistfully. A sadness unfolded from her, enveloping me, the barn, the world, the cosmos. An oceanic tear formed in the corner of just her left eye and plopped onto her outstretched leg. I was stunned; couldn't say a word, for a change. What was it about night crawlers that would evoke such sorrow from a creature at least five thousand times larger than they? I couldn't break her reverie to ask. I didn't need to.

"Imagine," she said softly, "the implications for the planet if human beings were sensitive to the nature of night crawlers?"

I thought of the story told through the centuries about Saint Francis moving worms out of the path of wagon wheels. "Yes," I replied.

"And night crawlers are only the beginning," she said, turning again to face me, light dancing across her wide and wonder-filled face. "Spiders, for example, have turquoise personalities for their preciseness and creativity. Songbirds are gold for their unbounded joy, while horses shimmer in a lovely silver for their swiftness of both foot and mind. Foxes, as you can imagine, come in as emerald for their sharp wit and good humor. Oh, did I mention the rats yet?"

"No," I said flatly. "But do tell me something wonderful about them, please?" The farm rats and I were in constant battle, it seemed, with the rats usually a full step ahead.

"Ah, the rat, the wonderful rat," Christina said with obvious respect, "has a personality that radiates a gorgeous, glowing orange, the epitome of mental acuity and perseverance, tempered with devotion for their own families, old and young alike. They will readily love and respect anyone who honestly demonstrates the same to them, no matter the species. And while they are quick to sense a deception, unlike your species, rats hold no grudges and seek no revenge."

"I thought nothing in nature held grudges," I replied.

"Precisely. That is why all the colors and tones of nature are so pure and radiant, but too often those of humans are muddied or dull."

The sun was now near to mid-sky and the mountains around us shimmered in the heat. Even the stones scattered outside the barn seemed to glow in a new way. Christina had once again sharpened my perceptions, guiding me into a wider and deeper consciousness, step by gentle step Yes, she had indeed told me something wonderful, not only about rats, but about life itself. I wondered if ladybugs were a B major and a red hue.

"Close," Christina replied to my thought. "Actually, they are a stunning magenta, for their incredibly positive outlook on life in general. By the way," she said sleepily, "Japanese iris purple-blue and sun-yellow are exceptionally complementary."

"Which means, we are..."

"Kindred spirits, my dear friend, kindred spirits."

And with those final words, Christina closed her eyes and turned her head back onto her shoulder for her noon nap. And I knew it was time for me to get back to my work. But I chose instead to lean against my warm and ample bovine, my teacher and my friend, and let our colors interblend—a fine miracle, indeed.

5   BE MY VALENTINE

BECAUSE OF OTHER OBLIGATIONS, THREE WEEKS WOULD PASS BEFORE I WAS able to once again search out my cow for more than the usual daily pleasantries. But the loss of a dear friend to cancer on a Tuesday in early October made me trudge through the gate in search of solace and wisdom. I found Christina in front of the barn, deeply involved in drawing an enormous heart with her nose. So complete was her concentration, at first she didn't notice me as I walked up beside her and stood quietly, admiring her work. What an elegant heart! A simple depiction of such a universal symbol, yet with all the appeal of the most ornate heart ever created. She blinked her long white eyelashes and swung her head toward me.

"What do you think?" she asked hopefully.

"Lovely," I replied. "But may I ask, why a heart?"

"It's a valentine," she stated.

While I tend to lose track of time, it seemed to me that we were eons from February the fourteenth. But to be polite, I asked, "A valentine for whom?"

Christina sighed heavily and once again studied her drawing in the dirt. "Earth," she said quietly. "She's having a rough go of it right now; I thought I would let her know I was thinking of her."

"That's thoughtful of you. Is it like a *card* for Earth?"

Christina didn't answer me. Instead, she began to walk around the heart, drawing a circle with her left hoof. When she returned to her original starting point, she looked skyward, closed her eyes, and pointed both her ears forward. "There," she said opening her eyes. "Delivered— and received. She was most grateful."

"What?" I asked, having gotten side tracked by a tinier-than-usual ladybug who had just landed on my arm.

"Not 'what'; *who*. Earth," Christina said rather sternly. Then she seemed to be listening intently. "Oh my goodness," she said, frowning once again. "I didn't mean to make her cry; I had no idea that she was such an emotional planet. Now there's a huge flood in Japan."

"Where?" I asked, still distracted. But Christina ignored me, so I decided to take a different approach to the subject. "What do you use for stamps?"

Christina turned and eyed me suspiciously. "Stamps? For what?"

"Valentine cards."

"Cows don't send Valentine cards."

"But..." Now I was *really* confused. "You just—"

"I send valentine heart expressgrams."

My grand and loving cow seemed to have lost patience with me, for she turned and started to walk up toward the back fence. I, however, still hot on the trail of knowledge, hurried after her, questions in tow. "What about the heart you drew? And the circle? And—"

"*Not* a card!" Christina mumbled through the air between us. She kept walking, increasing her pace. Feeling rejected, I stopped following her and watched her ample tail-end chug on away from me. Suddenly she stopped and looked back over her shoulder, dropping her head to stare at me in a most peculiar manner. "Well," she said, "are you coming along or not?" I threw my hands in the air and hurried to catch up to her. Once beside her, she continued her journey until she reached the far end of the pasture. There she stepped into the shade of a large Virginia pine and whumped her grand self down into a resting position.

"Here's the point," she said quietly, half-closing her eyes and accessing a wad of cud. "Or rather, I should say—here's the circle." She extended one leg forward and examined her hooves. "You are limiting yourself. You say you want inner peace. If so, you have to unbend that mind of yours and exist not from your brain, but from your heart."

I looked down at the place where I hoped my heart was safely tucked inside my chest.

"No, not your physical pump," Christina cried. "*Heart*, with a capital 'H'; *Love*, capital 'L'! Same thing—the kind of Heart/Love that has no borders or boundaries, that does not lay down any conditions or requirements; that has room for all, and then some, and always exists, even beyond time and space."

"And that has what to do with valentines and circles?" I asked.

"Everything."

"But... ?"

"The valentine is the Sacred Heart personified; the circle embraces and extends it to others. Kind of like conference-calling," said Christina. There was a long pause in our conversation. "And do you know why this is important?" she finally asked.

"No, I don't; not really," I said with a sigh.

"Because we care deeply about one another. Just as Earth and I care for each other." She watched me closely, knew I was hurting over the loss of my friend, but said nothing about it. "So, shall I draw you a valentine as well?" she asked quietly.

"That would be kind of you. I could use one."

Christina narrowed her eyes and looked sideways at me, jaws rotating over well-minced grass. I think she chuckled. "And you certainly deserve one—drawn in the dirt, sent to you by heart expressgram; in any and all ways, my pleasure," she said. "No delivery confirmation needed here. By the way," she added, "I sent one to the friend you just lost as well, to—you know... speed her on her way." She was thoughtful for a while; neither of us spoke until she looked over at me and said, "You know, I believe everyone deserves a valentine from time to time. Love is the most profound and pure energy that exists, the one constant in a sea of shifting illusion. Love comes from, and is received by, Heart, the center of all beings everywhere, not limited to or by—make note, please—form, species, or so-called animate/inanimate status."

My head was beginning to hurt; I found I was once again grieving for my friend. Christina studied me with immense compassion, then ever so softly asked me, "Will you be my valentine?"

I laughed. "Sure," I replied, rubbing her chin, her favorite tickle spot.

"Thank you," she said, "and I will be yours, if I may."

"Of course you can!"

"Then," my wise cow said, nodding her head in satisfaction, "you now understand that Heart (capital 'H') is not complicated at all. And in that Heart, you know exactly what I am talking about, because you already live that Love (capital 'L,' thank you), and that's what matters."

"Really?" I asked, once again busy tending to the little ladybug. She had flown off my arm to my knee, but landed upside down. I turned her right side up and wished her well as she flew off on the wind.

"Yes," Christina replied, watching me closely. "Really."

6   GETTING UNSTUCK

OCTOBER THAT YEAR WAS HOT AND MUGGY, NOT THE BEST OF CONDITIONS for slogging through chores such as shoveling manure and moving hay. But I was more concerned now about the declining health of my little fifteen-year-old donkey, Miso. Grief for him dominated my mind so much these days. And while I had never discussed him with Christina, certainly she must have observed my struggle to correct the terrible, benign cauliflower-type growths—called equine sarcoids—that affected his back right leg, his spine, and the base of one ear. I held tightly to my feelings and kept them deep inside of me.

On one particular morning, to make everything harder for me (or so it appeared), when I went to the barn for a piece of rope, I discovered the door to the feed shed was stuck tight as a tick. The sweat rolling down the back of my neck did nothing for my mood as I kicked the door a bit harder than necessary, trying to free it from its swollen jamb. In the adjoining stall Christina opened one sleepy eye, sighed dramatically, and studied me in her deadpan way.

"Sorry," I mumbled, as much to the door as to my cow.

"Bad day?" the cow (not the door) asked.

"Well, it ain't the easiest," I countered, continuing my battle with the door.

"Who said it was supposed to be easy? And don't use the word ain't."

I quit my assault on the door and turned to her. "Excuse me? So now you're the expert on English grammar?" Of course, I already knew she was, but I was not about to admit it.

"The correct term, my dear companion, would be 'grammar-ian,' unless, of course, one prefers to employ the Greek derivative, in which case *grammatikos* would be more appropriate." She reached down, selected a piece of leafy hay, and proceeded to give it her full attention. I couldn't help but laugh. Sure, it was rude, but a cow correcting my grammar? I wasn't in the mood. "I'll use *ain't* if I want to," I retaliated.

"Suit yourself; it's a free universe." She closed her eyes, ignoring my impertinence.

"Look here, Christina," I began, realizing my voice was rising, "I was only using the word for emphasis; I *am* a college graduate, you know."

Her Cowness opened her eyes halfway again, while her jaws remained in perfect rotation on her cud. "Correct grammatical usage shows respect for your language, enhances the power of the spoken *and* written word, and thereby has the capability of being a most remarkable tool for healing. Believe me—the planet needs all the healing she can get."

"But..."

"And careless or rude speech is only destructive. Make your choice; I believe I've heard you say you want to help heal others?"

"But..." My words trailed off because I knew she was right; I had no argument left. More than anything, I wanted to help others—especially the animals—heal, not only here at my own small sanctuary, but everywhere. And right at that particular moment I was especially sensitive on the subject because of Miso.

Christina stirred. She knew my thoughts. Bless her, she always saw past my temperamental ways. And as usual, her manner was understanding yet firm, neither sharp nor judgmental. After all, her job was to teach me; we both knew that.

"Care to talk about it?" she ventured, rising to her feet. She began her leisurely stretch: front feet forward, her massive back slightly bowed, and her gloriously long tail wound in a tight circle high up on her back. While it was good to forget about that door for a moment, I knew I had to get into the shed, and the door was not helping me. I sat down on the ground and wiped the sweat away from my eyes.

"Dang humidity," I mumbled. "Can't see straight with it all over my face."

Christina extended her left foot and delicately licked her ankle. That would mean, *Excuse me for pointing this out, but you're incorrect—again.*

"What did I say wrong now?" I asked.

Christina tilted her head to the side and looked at me, her eyes narrowed. "It's not because of the sweat that you can't see well," she said gently. "It's frustration that's got you stuck, just like the door."

"The door is frustrated?" Now I was confused.

"I'm talking about Miso, and ultimately, one's ability to heal."

"And I shouldn't be frustrated?" I demanded. "Nothing works on those wretched growths from a medical standpoint, and he won't let me do anything herbally or homeopathically. He fights all my attempts to help him."

Christina ambled away from me, checking clumps of grass here and there. Usually that meant our conversation was over, leaving me in even greater frustration. I had hoped that perhaps she could solve Miso's problem.

"That's Miso's job," she offered from the depths of a dandelion plant.

"What?" I said, leaning in her direction. "I didn't hear—"

"Exactly," she said with perfect enunciation, despite the remains of mangled plant particles drooping from her mouth. "You *don't* hear him."

Confused, exhausted, and sweaty, I slumped back down on the ground under the maple tree, allowing its strong trunk to support my sad self. I really just wanted to sleep and forget the whole thing, but now that the subject had been opened, I knew Christina would not permit me to just walk away from it.

"Healing involves not only listening, but also knowing when to yield," she said, settling down beside me. I could feel her warm breath on my ear and knew she had much to say. Of course, it would all be grammatically correct.

"I do that," I said defensively. "When I pray for someone's healing, I always add, 'Thy will be done.' If that isn't yielding..."

"Not God's will; in this case, *Miso's* will. You can't expect him to heal if he isn't ready, or doesn't even want to be healed at all."

"And why wouldn't he want to get better?" I asked. The growths on his ear were large and obstructive, and their periodic spells of bleeding caused flies and gnats to constantly worry him. It was terrible to watch him when he was so uncomfortable.

"Rarely is one ready to be healed even when the so-called affliction seems at its worst," Christina replied. "Until one is willing to let go of the mental or emotional aspect, the physical manifestation will remain. And Miso is hanging on tightly to his."

"Which is?"

"Among other things, worry. Mostly he's worried about you. He's become increasingly overprotective of you and thinks you work too hard."

"So his condition is my fault?"

"No. His emotions and thoughts are his own. That's why he has to change them. And part of your task is to listen to what he needs to do. When you are trying to help another heal, whether physically, emotionally, or spiritually, if you have to struggle or fight to get their cooperation, or the condition is unresponsive to your work, then it's not yet time for that healing to occur."

Now I felt helpless as well. "So, do I stop trying to help him?"

"No; step back and listen to what he is trying to tell you about what he needs from you, and from himself."

Muffling sound coming from behind us. A short snort followed, and I turned to see Miso leaning over the fence, studying us intently. I thought of all my own health concerns, enough to fill an entire medical journal. Yes, indeed, I wanted to be completely well, but apparently not enough, or I would take better care of myself—I would listen to my own inner dialogue. It seemed I had attitudes I wasn't ready to let go of yet. I was as stuck as that barn door.

"I see your point," I said.

"Just remember," Christina said quietly. "Help where and when you can; if there is resistance, back up. It isn't time. And there is neither shame nor wrongness nor guilt involved—ever. What is, simply—is. Always move forward; never look back."

Christina tucked her head back over her shoulder, politely indicating that she wanted to sleep. Miso turned from the fence and joined my other donkeys, Nori and Julia, as they walked off to graze in the honeysuckle. For right now, this one warm October day, Miso seemed stable and oddly enough, content.

I tried to see a lesson in all of this for myself, but in fact, I was fighting away tears, feeling as if I was not very good at anything. Even grammar, and I, a published author! Grammar reminded me of my need to get that shed door open. As I rose to my feet and tiptoed back to the barn, I heard a pronounced sigh from the grass, followed by a polite cough.

"Don't be so tough on yourself," Christina said, never opening her eyes. "You're doing a fine job here, a really fine job. Now, politely ask that door to help you, and it will."

I approached the shed door and did just that—in a most agreeable and friendly manner. Then I reached for the handle and the door opened, effortlessly.

I heard Christina chuckle: "Now ain't that something!"

PHOTO BY JO BRAKE.

7   LIVING WITH GANDHI

CHRISTINA TOOK A BURDOCK LEAF FROM MY HAND AND CHEWED it thoughtfully, then spit it out. "Limp," she said.

"Limp?" I replied, offended. I had chosen my gift carefully as the most succulent among so many other leaves already old and withered by October's first frost.

"Yup. Limp." She punctuated her opinion of my offering with a low and rumbly burp. "It's quite all right," she continued, perhaps assuming I intended to apologize. But my ego refused to be so polite. So the leaf was less than perfect; who among us on this Earth is perfect?

"I didn't say the leaf was less than perfect," my rotund and profound cow answered, once again reading my thoughts. "Everything is perfect. Eventually, though, things in physical bodies get to be a bit, well... limp."

Oh, could I relate.

Christina yawned.

I poked the pitchfork in the roll of hay and dragged off a sizable bunch for her dinner. As I shoved the hay in the corner of her stall, I felt a new wave of exhaustion hit me in my shoulders, then seep up to my head and down to my toes. Without any other warning, depression pressed down on me until my legs wanted to buckle to the ground. Sweat poured out of my skin, chilling my body even in the strong afternoon sun, and nausea twisted my stomach. Christina shifted her eyes from the inviting pile of hay to my face, and without a word, waited for me to regain my senses. After a while she said softly, "You're stuck again; you're just denying your grief."

I knew she must be right; she always is. Miso wasn't the first creature in my family to have caused me ongoing concern. Having recently lost my little, ancient dog, Gremi, a gray and black poodle-terrier mix whom I adopted five years earlier. I was once again overwhelmed in my mind, my heart, certainly my soul, and now, it seemed, my body as well. But at that particular moment when I could barely remain upright, I was not interested in her lectures. Being a compassionate cow, she did not respond, but simply let me stagger on with my chores. I put more hay in for the goats, closed the feed room, and opened her gate. Only then did she speak.

"You miss Gremi. Say it aloud. Scream! Beat the ground! Cry till your eyes puff up. Then see if all that doesn't help you."

"Doesn't exactly sound appealing," I replied grimly. Sometimes her lectures made me cross. "Sure I miss Gremi. She was a special little dog; but she was old, and it was her time to go. Besides, I know she's in a good place now." But even as the words left my mouth, I felt the dry emptiness behind them. Too stubborn to admit defeat, I chattered on. "So what do you know about losing someone special?" I asked. As she had been with me since she was a small calf, I was sure the death of another was not part of her experience. Oh, was I wrong.

Christina lowered her head, and a single tear fell from each eye. "My mother," she whispered, "was taken away." I could easily guess where her mother had been taken. I wrapped my arms around her enormous neck.

"I am so sorry," I said, burying my face into her sweet-smelling coat. "I didn't mean to be so insensitive."

Christina snuffled appreciatively and set about eating her hay. "It's all right," she said. "My mother had a path to follow, as did I. I was meant to come here to protect and teach you." We looked at each other for several minutes with an even deeper mutual respect than we'd had before. When she spoke again, her voice was strong: "So if you don't want to vent in such a dramatic manner, may I suggest delving into your heart's memory and recalling all the grand, loving, happy, wise, spirited aspects of your little dog?"

I assured her that I didn't feel strong enough to engage in either of her suggestions. In fact, I felt completely stampeded by everything in my life lately, and despite the day's long list of Things Yet to Do, I curled up in the soft grass beside her stall and let the late-day sun warm my aching bones. Could grief really cause all those nightmarish symptoms I was experiencing? They had started two weeks before, just after Gremi died, and had continued almost daily since then.

Despite my objections, as I closed my eyes and my frantic brain started to relax, Gremi appeared in my mind. She looked straight at me, with that direct, loving gaze that clearly reflected her expansive soul. Pure, luminescent light seemed to pour from her, as if she were composed of iridescent pearl. The vision of her held steady, even when a large, very broad, and moist pink nose nuzzled my face. Christina wished to speak.

"Okay. Sure, go ahead," I whispered to her. I didn't want to lose contact with what I sensed was Gremi's spirit. But I also knew Christina would not interrupt so important a visit without good reason.

"Tell me about Gremi," my beloved bovine said quietly.

"Well," I began, "living with Gremi was like living with Gandhi. From the day she came to live here when she was nine, until she died two weeks ago at fourteen, she was always the peacekeeper among the dogs."

"How so?" Christina asked.

"Gremi never growled at anyone. She never snapped at or bit anyone, except me once, and the doctor once, the day before she died. She was in a lot of pain. Even then she didn't bite down. I remember when I picked her up, she gently wrapped her teeth around my hand as if to say, *Please don't do that; my stomach hurts.* That was the only way she had of letting us know."

I paused, falling into despair that this little dog should have ever felt pain.

"Please tell me more," Christina urged.

"Okay," I replied, sniffling into my tissue. "Gremi could run like the wind. Sometimes it seemed as if she ran just *above* the ground, with her feet suspended in midair. When she would run like that, I knew she felt really well."

"She didn't always feel well, did she?" Christina asked. Obviously she knew all the answers, but I gave them to her anyway. It felt comforting to me to talk about my little friend.

"No, she didn't," I replied. "She often had problems with her stomach, and she was blind and deaf on her right side because of a serious head trauma when she was young." *Sometimes just getting through the day seemed impossible for me,* Gremi's spirit said to me, *but you were always there to help me. After I came to live with you, I never suffered.*

Again, Gremi's image began to glow in my mind, and her eyes sparkled with life, letting me know how infinitely healthy and happy she was now in the realm of spirit, and how immortal our love for each other would always be.

"What about the hot dog rolls?" Christina asked.

"Oh, yes!" I began to laugh as Gremi's spirit danced in happy circles. *Even the thought of hot dog rolls gives me joy,* she was saying to me, *even though I'm no longer able to enjoy the Earth-bound kind.*

"Gremi," I began, "loved bread, any kind, but mostly that white, gummy stuff. And best of all, she loved hot dog rolls, preferably top-sliced. Pepperidge Farm brand, of course. I would sit on the bed and she would stand on the floor next to me. When I tapped on the side of the bed, she would jump up, put her front paws on the edge of the quilt, and look expectantly for her piece of bread. When I gave it to her, she would hop down again, eat the bread, and wait for me to pat the quilt again. We would do this until she had eaten the entire roll. We had such a good time!"

By the time I'd finished my description, I was laughing, tears flowing freely down my face. For in my vision of her, she was running in circles and playing, letting me know how much our time together had meant to her. *It's a memory,* she said to me, *that will remain precious to me forever.* I couldn't have agreed more.

And then I was aware of Christina who, had she been able to, would have been dancing as well. Her eyes shone as brightly as those of Gremi's spirit, and I suddenly realized that Christina had been seeing Gremi's spirit as well.

"Gremi is right here with us and will be for as long as you need her," Christina whispered. "You see, you have not lost her at all."

As I turned to look at Christina, Gremi's image faded from my mind. Yet I knew she had not disappeared, only moved temporarily from my sight. I noticed that my exhaustion was gone, along with all of my physical and emotional pain. In different times, other dimensions, I probably would have started chewing cud, I felt so centered and relaxed.

8   PERFECT PEACE

"CUD," SHE SAID, "IS YOUR TRUTH."

"Okay," I responded, still feeling happy. "If you say so." I wasn't sure it didn't matter now; peace was mine.

"For the moment," Christina countered, studying my thoughts. I must have frowned because she raised her head up and looked down at me with intense eyes. "Human beings," she continued, "have a tendency to become de-centered and off-balanced rather easily. For example, *if* I were to tell you that the Weather Channel was calling for severe thunderstorms..."

Immediately my heart began to race. Storms themselves fascinate me, but I have an enormous fear that lightning may strike one of my animals or burn down the barn. Yes, *de-centered* would be a mild term for my sudden and intense distress.

"There are no storms predicted; nonetheless, I think I've made my point," Christina said. "Now, I am going to give you a tool of immense value. Share it with everyone you know, and even those you don't. The more you share this tool, the greater will be its value. And you will never need to fear thunderstorms or anything else ever again. Anger, judgment, resentment, defending, or offending will no longer even occur to you. It will freely give you everything you seek regarding inner peace. But you will need to practice constantly. Now, listen carefully." She shifted her weight, then spoke in the kindest of tones. "There can be no greater peace than this: to know that you are love, and in your gratitude for everything that overflows your heart, offer your love back out into the world. And guaranteed—all beings, including storms, who like you are also love, will respond in kind." She continued to look at me while hardly blinking, so focused was she on my face. Her simple declaration stunned me with its intensity and implications. The very sound of the words seemed to project an energy that was transformative to everything with which they came in contact, like light meeting an object and illuminating it.

"Love," she continued softly, closing her eyes as she spoke, "is for all moments—this one, the next one, forever. It has no boundaries and no schedules to follow. Love lives within the heart of all beings. It is what will keep you and Gremi, you and Miso, you and everyone else you have cared for—or will care for in the future—closely connected beyond time and space. Love, in its truest sense, is your truth; it is who you are."

"And cud?" I asked, confused by her opening statement.

"Cud nourishes, energizes, centers, grounds, and eventually replenishes the Earth. It is the manifestation of love, in its purest form, in action. Cud is, in a word, perfect, like love in its more sacred nature."

It had not been an easy day for me—so many extremes of emotion, as well as physical symptoms. I thought perhaps it was time for my own dinner and a cup of tea...

9   DOING TIME
WITH CHRISTINA

BUT AT THAT PRECISE MOMENT, CHRISTINA TURNED HER HEAD DOWN TO STARE fixedly at her left front ankle. "Just as I thought," she mumbled. "According to my watch, I'm already late."

"And that would be late for what?" I asked, not blinking an eye. Who was I to bring up the fact that I didn't see any watch strapped above her hoof; and anyway, what use would a cow have for a watch? Most likely this was, once again, her unique way of provoking me into a necessary life lesson. *Just doing my job*, she would say to me. Of course, being able to read my thoughts, she knew what my brain was mulling over, but she chose to ignore it.

"Darn if it isn't already spring in Australia, and I forgot to send that birthday gift," she mumbled.

"And to whom would that be?" I asked smoothly.

Christina looked up from her appendage with obvious annoyance. Rarely did I see her so flustered. Had she really messed up this time, forgetting to send whatever it was, to whomever, in Australia?

"No, not in *Australia*," she said crossly, catching my thought in midair. "The gift was for Jacquelyn in Paris."

Sadly, I fell for it all and was hooked. "And that has *what* to do with spring Down Under?" Instantly, I regretted asking. Christina glanced at her ankle again. She appeared to be chewing her cud rather aggressively. "It's complicated."

"Obviously," I replied. I returned to my task of picking burdock off my sweater.

"But if you must know...," she said, as much to her foot as to me.

"Not really. I don't have time."

"Oh," she said, as if she had lost her only friend.

"Well," I said, pointedly looking at *my* watch-less wrist, "I guess I have a minute to spare." I was beginning to have real suspicions now regarding her intent in all of this. But she did look desperately pathetic.

Christina sighed dramatically and sank to the ground with a 1,400-pound (give or take) *THUNK*. Her earlier agitation had disappeared and now she merely looked despondent. Cud ceased its eternal journey from stomach chamber to stomach chamber to stomach chamber to stomach chamber (yes, there are four), and even the fly-groupies on her back sighed.

"You *never* have time..." she began sadly.

"I have a full life."

"... to just sit and chat anymore," she said, adding, "I miss that." The massive head drooped three inches, but I thought I caught one eye peeking up at me from under her impossibly long lashes. Nonetheless, guilt grabbed me hard. Was I whining pitifully? "I just don't have enough *time* for everything," I said.

Christina extended her front left leg and again admired the absentee watch above her ankle. "Oh, I don't buy that one," she replied quietly. "Time is all in your mind."

I was afraid to ask for clarity; didn't need to. She was, once again, on a roll. Life lesson number 97.

"Time is the creation of the human brain. It applies only to the physical world and the workings of the human animal. In and of itself, time is fictional. We, of the natural world, have neither need for, nor concept of time as you perceive it."

"Yes you do!" I said defensively. Suddenly I felt as inferior as I had always guessed us humans to be. But I wasn't going down without a fight. "You know when it's time to eat, or rest, or graze..."

"None of those are *clock*-oriented, but light- and enzyme-directed, instinctual. And, we listen to our inner voice, you know—where perfect Love resides. In our world, there's not a clock face or calendar to be found." Christina sighed happily, and burped, indicating that peace was returning to her furrowed brow. "Do you know how silly time has become?" she said, settling down again. "So the sun is high in the sky right now. Why give it a number on a clock? It's midday, warm, and lovely. Just enjoy it. So the leaves are falling off the trees and the turtles are going into hibernation. Isn't that enough to tell you what season it is? Why attach a month— a name—to it?"

"But doing so helps us know where we're at, and when we have to be somewhere." My gut instinct told me that my point was as limp as the burdock leaf. Besides, Christina was relentless.

"Give me an example," Christina said.

"Okay. 'Oh, look, it's six o'clock. I have to feed the dogs now!' How was that?"

"Weak," Christina replied. "Try this: 'Look at the dogs—they're jumping around your feet. They're *killing* each other. Their blood sugar must be low. The sun is setting. So go feed the dogs."

"All right; how about dentist appointments; publication deadlines; what time is the plumber coming to fix the leaking pipes?"

Christina didn't waste a second. "Eat properly, you won't need a dentist. Publications reach people who need them, precisely when they are needed—let the universe handle the details; and plumbers never show up when they say they will."

Couldn't argue with that. But, of course, I had to try.

"What's wrong with using a clock, with having time as a guideline?"

Christina looked patiently at me, with that *Someday maybe she'll understand expression.* "There isn't anything wrong with time at all, but, my dear, as with so many things humans touch, time—a potentially valuable tool—is too often abused, given more importance than it deserves. It can even become a weapon."

"Such as?"

"*Ten years to life,* for starters. 'Your *time* has run out.' 'It's *time* you learned your lesson / the truth / who's boss / you get what's coming to you...' 'Are you some kind of idiot? How many *times* do I have to tell you...' 'I wouldn't give him the *time* of day...' "

There wasn't anything to say in reply that was cute or smart or clever, or that would take away the awful sting of her truth. How could we humans abuse such a simple concept as time and twist it so grotesquely?

"How frequently do you bemoan the fact that you 'don't have

enough time?' " Christina said, more softly now, "and turn away oppor-
tunities to have lunch with a friend, or a nap in the afternoon sun? What
presses so hard on you that the clock ticks on and you are always chasing
it, filled with regrets?"

"But," I replied feebly, "our lives are so much more complicated
than yours, or a tree's, for goodness' sake. You don't have to shop
for your food, or meet deadlines, or earn money just to exist, or keep
up a house."

"And you don't get made into hamburger, or milled into lumber."

"*What's that got to do with time?*" I wailed in frustration.

But Christina just hunkered down in the cool autumn grass and
contemplated her cloven toes. Thoughts of missed birthday gifts seemed
to have vanished. Even unbearable images of factory farming faded from
her face. She was all serenity.

"What I am demonstrating, my dear student," she said calmly, "is
that we all have issues—whether we are human, tree, cow, or bee. Ever
hear a tree say, 'My *time* is up! Here comes the man with a chain saw'? Or
a cow bemoan, 'I have so little *time* left; I go to market next week,' or the
bee: "It's September fourteenth and I haven't finished my hive yet!' The
answer is no, you don't, and you never will. We live moment to moment,
fully aware of the preciousness of all that is.

"Yes, our instincts remind us of when to eat and rest, when to grow
leaves or new coats or gather pollen—whatever is appropriate to the individual species. But we don't rush around wringing our branches, hooves,
feet, or stingers because we are too late, or too early, or not getting it all
done 'on time.' Do you understand?"

Sitting in the afternoon sun, on a perfect October day. Methodically
plucking sticky burrs from my sweater. Enjoying a lively and intriguing
sparring match with my massive companion. Recognizing the honor she
gave me by sharing her wisdom. Noticing how the touch of wind hinted
at winter approaching. Feeling the tickle of coarse grass through my jeans.
Knowing—absolutely—the perfection of everything around me in that
precise moment. Yes, I understood.

"Well, it's about *time* you did!" Christina declared, cud caught in a
chuckle. And then there was that silly cow, glancing at her left front ankle
again. "Well, will you look at that," she said. "It's *time* for my soap opera,
As the Hay Bales. If you will excuse me, I'd better hurry or I'll be *late* for
the good part."

Surely I was staring incredulously, because my cow, my unbelievably wicked cow, was laughing hysterically. I, on the other hand, felt a strong need not for tea anymore, but for chocolate. Before I reached the kitchen door I turned, because I had to know: "And what then was all that about your supposed watch, and spring in Australia, and a friend in Paris?"

"Oh *that*," she replied, flicking her tail in such a casual manner. "That was just to get your attention. Actually, Jacquelyn lives in London..."

10   POINT TWO

THURSDAY PRODUCED THE FIRST COLD MORNING OF NOVEMBER. Those early hours were cumbersome: wearing jacket and gloves for the first time in months, dealing with frozen toes and a sniffly nose... I hurried through morning barn chores, forgetting, in my self-absorption, something of great importance. Apparently, all the animals knew I had done so, yet Christina, normally the spokescow for all, stood silently in front of her gate, waiting for the sun to emerge. She watched me shuffle the shovel around various deposits of cow and donkey manure, clearly communicating a message to me through those strong dark eyes. But I missed it. Only when I piled fresh hay high in her stall did she cough politely and shift her front feet, a pointed way of bringing my attention to the present.

"What?" I asked, thinking ahead to the warm kitchen and hot, buttered toast waiting for me. In response, she flickered her left ear back and forth in such a deliberate manner, I should have noticed. Still, I missed my cue.

"Chickens have such a tenuous way of getting one's attention," she said quietly, the ear still in motion.

"And that has to do with *what?*" I replied, as I closed and hooked the pasture gate.

Christina turned her nose down toward a smallish, quite ruffled form standing patiently by the fence, then back up to stare at me. "Oh good grief; my poor Rosetta!" I mumbled as I hurried back to the feed room for a handful of shelled corn. "How could I possibly forget your treat?" The aged Rhode Island Red hen tilted her head to one side as I approached, and she began to murmur in a most endearing manner. I loved her dearly, as I have adored all the chickens who have graced my family sanctuary over the years. I felt sad to have overlooked her. "Hens are so patient and polite," Christina continued from behind me. "So misunderstood by humans in general, eh?"

I waved my hand to cut her off. I do try to not interrupt her vast wisdom, but at the moment she needed to know her usually pink nose was turning blue from the chilly air. I suggested we retreat to the stall. Perhaps her ears were too cold as well, because she said "What?" and then, presumably reading my mind, backed into the barn. She poked tentatively through her hay pile, selecting a mouthful of dried clover and orchard grass and rolling it around in her mouth with as much finesse as if she were an experienced wine taster from the heart of France. After allowing a full minute to allow the digestive juices to charge into full gear, she swung her head back in my direction, carefully enunciating four short words: "See—you—at—noon."

What to do now but conclude my work there and head back into the house to feed the dogs. I didn't mind Christina setting the schedule, but perhaps she could have added, "Would it be convenient for you if we continued this conversation at noon?" Or, "Do you mind if we continue this discussion over lunch? Shall we say, noonish?" Nonetheless, noon it was when I strode out the back door to find her reclining in the now-warmed air. Her long, glorious tail flicked across her back, sending clouds of tiny flies spinning off her like so many satellites.

I snuggled down next to her and chewed on a toothpick. "I just found out my book contract's falling through," I said sadly. "And I was already planning what to wear to my first book signing. Reminds me of a saying I learned when I was growing up about not counting your chickens before they hatch."

"Which brings me back around to the fowl of the world," Christina remarked in satisfaction. It was as if we had not been apart for the past five hours. "And I would recommend reconsidering such a statement if I were you."

"What?" I countered. The word what seemed to be popping up a lot in the day's conversations. Funny how things come in clusters.

"Indeed," Christina remarked, reading my thoughts. As usual, I felt uncomfortable about this habit of hers.

"No need to," she said. "You send quite distinctive visual images—picture thoughts; they're hard to miss. I was merely commenting on that one."

"I beg your pardon?" I said, after carefully avoiding the word what.

"Well, there are all these little clusters of what's floating around in your head. I was merely commenting—"

"Yes, yes, I know, but get back to the chickens," I said, desperately wanting to change the subject.

Christina seemed to have completed her round with the morning's clover and had decided to ruminate for a while on the remainders of some dried maple leaves. Gas rumbled deep within her four-chambered stomach, finally emerging through closed teeth. I noticed her nose had returned to a charming pink.

"It is my opinion," she began, "based on lengthy observation and much interviewing of the creatures in question, that chickens are victims of bad press and fast-food chains, all of which falsely and unfairly assign this most remarkable bird to a station of negligible stature."

I stared at her for a long time, and she appeared to relish it, for she knew I was finally stumped for a smart reply.

"Absolutely," she continued without haste, knowing she had the edge. "Chickens actually far outrank the most educated of the human elite in terms of gray matter. Brain stuff. Intellect."

"I get your point," I agreed. "But most people consider chickens to have very small brains."

"Size has nothing to do with intelligence," she replied quickly. "For example, a wasp is incredibly intelligent, as are ants and certain beetles. Yet, to the untrained they appear to be merely pests. On the other hand, the supposedly most intelligent, yet, in fact deadliest animal on Earth is—"

She knew I could finish that one: "Man."

She bowed her head. "Precisely."

"But what about chickens?" I was losing patience; I had things to do.

"Rosetta proves an interesting point here," Christina said evenly, ignoring the edge in my voice. "Rather than get *impatient*"—and she emphasized the word while leaning in close to my face—"she waited by the fence this morning, hoping you would remember her corn. On the other hand, she communicated quite distinctly to me that should you forget her, it would neither destroy her, nor her day. In so many words. I believe she said it a bit differently." Christina was getting wordy again, a sign that she felt she was not getting through to me, her star (and only) pupil.

"I know I overlook her sometimes," I said with honest humility. "And I always feel bad about it. I try, I really do try to remember everything and everyone around here." Suddenly, my mood shifted to defensive. "Ever hear of overload? Burnout?"

"WHAT??" Christina replied, her eyes wide in pretended seriousness. I laughed, and the chill that I had started between us, broke.

"My point, dear friend," she continued, "is that hens understand and practice cosmic rules that reach beyond what smacks of apparent limitation. Point One: Had you forgotten Rosetta's snack this morning, she would have been—how would you say it?—okay with it. That's called living from your Heart. For her—no large deal. And Point Two..."

"Big."

"*What?*" she asked, genuinely startled this time.

"Big. The phrase is *big* deal, not *large* deal."

Christina sighed in exasperation. "Then perhaps I can clarify my point," she said, swallowing her cud for the forty-third time, "by saying that Rosetta was not bound by expectation or judgment."

But *I* was. The afternoon was drifting away and I had obligations. I thought it expedient to reintroduce the topic of not counting chickens...

"Lilly is a prime example," Christina replied, jumping straight to the center of my thoughts, just as I expected.

"What about Lilly?" I asked. "And what is Point Two?" I really wanted to know because Lilly was one of my favorites. She was my little bantam hen, imported from a kind farmer to keep Rosetta company after Rosetta's sister had died some weeks back. But early on in the relationship, Lilly had decided to go broody and hatch an egg. Problem was, with no rooster on the place, the egg would never hatch, and Rosetta, left alone again, abandoned ship (coop) and returned to live with the duck flock. Meanwhile, Lilly, determined that her egg would hatch, sat and sat and sat and sat...

"And then?" Christina prodded. She knew, of course, but wanted me to tell the story. An audience had gathered around me: not only the usual fly-groupies, but also several beetles, three ants, a handful of crickets, and a worm. A crow teetered intently on the branch above us. I suddenly felt very important.

"Okay," I said dramatically. "I was kindly given some more hens and a rooster, and one of the hens, a Buff Orpington, laid an egg on one of the nesting boxes next to Lilly's. Since we now had a rooster (although he was still very young), just in case the egg was fertilized, I shoved it under Lilly—more to give her something to do after her egg rotted, than anything else. I really doubted the second egg would hatch either." I paused here and drew in a long breath for effect. It worked: my audience leaned forward in anticipation.

"And then?" Christina coaxed again.

"Sadly, my rooster died of unknown causes a week later."

"And then?" she persisted, as if stuck in a groove, but anxious to hear the climax to the story she already knew.

"Well, eventually, about forty days after Lilly started sitting on her first egg, and precisely twenty-one days after she adopted the second egg, suddenly there was a yellow puff with a tiny beak, peeking out from under her!"

"So, the second egg—"

"Hatched." I finished Christina's line with relish. I'm sure everyone in the crowd around us applauded.

"And the moral is?" my cow-teacher asked.

"That persistence pays off?"

"Okay," she countered, "and?"

"If you hold something strongly enough in your heart, it will happen?"

"Not bad for a beginner," my now-beaming cow replied. "And what does that tell you?"

"Oh, what the heck—go ahead and count your chickens before they hatch!" I hollered out with glee. "By any chance, would that be Point Two?"

"Yes! Yes!" bellowed Christina, thrilled that her student was finally making progress. It had to be any teacher's finest moment. "Just think," she said, with emphasis to all those gathered around us, "of the implications, the possibilities of having precisely what you want in your life. After all, if it worked for Lilly..."

My dear cow was suddenly overcome with the enormity of it all, leaning back on the grass to play out all the angles of such a concept in her massive brain (but remember, size is not important). The crow flew off to spread the word; the beetles and worm, ants, crickets, and flies all scattered to tell their friends. The entire neighborhood was abuzz with the news. And all it took was one wise cow, a very stubborn and brainy hen named Lilly, and her elderly ex-companion, the infinitely patient Rosetta, to set world opinion straight (at least for a moment) on two issues: Point One—chickens are really pretty cool creatures who appreciate love, both the giving and receiving of it. And Point Two? Sometimes it's okay to throw away caution and count your chickens, in whatever form they come, especially for something you hold dear to you and believe in strongly. Then it is part of the truth of who you already are, no matter how strange or nonsensical that truth may seem to anyone else. A useful lesson ready for the testing.

11   UNCOMMON WINGS

BECAUSE—THE VERY NEXT MORNING THE TEMPERATURES ONCE again warmed up substantially, following a night of heavy rain, causing mud to slide unabashedly into the crack in my right sneaker and invade my sock. Not the best way to start a day. This messy event produced a lengthy diatribe from me about victimization even as Truth and Love sank beneath my numerous complaints. These, in turn, finally dissolved into something about needing a new pair of shoes. Totally self-absorbed, I was unaware of a bulky cow leaning over my shoulder. When the bulkiness spoke, I tipped forward, landing full-square in the rain puddle that had started it all.

"So do I," Her Cowness declared, pondering her cloven feet.

"So do you *what?*" I managed to spit out between globs of mud.

"Need new shoes," she replied without hesitation.

"You don't wear shoes," I said through clenched teeth, climbing out of the slop.

Obviously unconcerned with my accident, Christina cranked her massive head around to study her back toes. "Yes, I do," she said deliberately.

"NO YOU DON'T!" I practically shrieked. Then I toned it down a notch: "*Cows don't wear shoes.*"

Christina stared at me with a confused look that would have caused a furrowing of her brows, had she had any. "Oh. You mean you haven't seen my shoes?" She was genuinely incredulous. Over our many years of close friendship and more recent months of conversing with one another, I had come to learn how to distinguish Christina the Prankster from Christina the Truth Hawker. No question; this time she wasn't giving me any bull.

"So," I said, deciding to ride this one to the end, "where are your shoes?"

Christina shifted uncomfortably from one side to the other. She had that now-I'm-getting-worried-about-her expression in her eyes, when they kind of wince up a bit and her left ear pivots backwards, twice.

"Well, I'm not wearing any at the *moment...*"

"Exactly!" I was triumphant. That would be Rita: one, Christina: zero. Match point.

"Because my last pairs wore out..."

"What?"

"And that's why I need new ones."

I opened my mouth, but nothing came out. Scratch the previous score. It was, quite obviously, Rita: zero; Christina: four, one for each of her silly shoeless feet. I excused myself from Her Presence and retreated to the house, where a hot shower, clean overalls, and a fulfilling breakfast soothed my disheveled nerves. I decided a fresh cup of coffee would set things right, put matters into perspective—perhaps. One could never fully count on normalcy with Christina.

But after all, what was normal about anything these days? Here it was, mid-November, and it was 72 degrees outside. Hollyhocks would be reemerging in the garden, the dogs would begin to shed out months ahead of schedule, and flies, bees, and mosquitoes were bound to return with all the vigor of spring's rebirth. And now my cow wanted shoes. No, sorry—correction: *new* shoes. The thought of where she had put her old ones began to overtake my brain. Maybe if she could produce the old pairs I would be able to come to terms with this in a pragmatic and intellectual fashion—what human beings need. So with that optimistic thought I hastened out to her yard to find her conversing with a newly awakened black and purple hornet.

"It's been a while since Virginia had weather like this," Christina was saying, exchanging pleasantries with her visitor. The hornet tucked her wings across her back with all the finesse of a dancer and coughed politely.

"Wouldn't right remember," she said, "since we hornets only live for a year."

"No past-life recall?" Christina inquired with a chuckle. The hornet, obviously a creature with a strong sense of humor, laughed so hard she lost her balance, pitching forward. Fortunately for her there was no puddle for her to fall into. If there had been, it occurred to me that my compassionate cow would have asked me to help clean the mud from the small one, give her a hearty breakfast of whatever it is hornets long for, and most likely provide a clean pair of—yup!—shoes.
I just sighed.

"Am I intruding?" I asked, sitting across from the two of them.

The hornet edged back nervously, but Christina immediately reassured her.

"Not to worry; this person is my friend. She would never hurt you."

The hornet looked unconvinced. "No insecticide?" she asked, peering around as if to see what I might have hidden behind my back.

"None," I said, spreading my hands in an open, yielding gesture.

"Oh," she said flatly. I could sense she still didn't trust me.

"No insecticide, fly traps, sticky paper, or swatters." I had run out of insect murder weapons. But apparently, in her one year on Earth, she had learned one more possibility, from direct experience, no doubt. Studying my feet, she asked cautiously: "What about your shoes?"

So, what was all this about shoes today? Were the stars in some sort of alignment, or was the sun linked to something of a planetary nature? *"What's wrong with my shoes?"* I said. I guess I sounded a bit hostile, for the hornet backed rapidly into the protective custody of Christina's tail.

"No, no, no!" Christina hastily interrupted. "She wants to know if you plan to use your shoe to bash her. It's a common practice among your species, you know."

By this time the little creature was hidden further behind Christina's tail, poking an anxious face in my direction just in case I became violent. Instead, I suddenly began to see the absurdity of it all and just... grew... silent.

"My sweet friend," I began at last, getting down on eye level with the trembling hornet. "My shoes, leaky though they are, are not objects of destruction. They protect my feet from cold weather, rocks, and if God is good, mud. I would no more consider bashing you with my shoe—"

"—than I would with mine," Christina completed triumphantly.

"Excuse me?" the hornet asked hesitantly. That's when I was to learn just how much the pint-sized creature and I had in common, because there she was, boldly coming forth from Christina's tail and staring at those (yes, shoeless) cloven hooves. "But I don't see any, ummm, shoes," she ventured.

"You don't?" Christina said, winking at me.

"Uh, no," the hornet replied. Despite her fear of me, I noticed that the hornet was edging toward me, studying Christina most carefully. "I didn't know cows wore shoes."

"Of course we do!" Christina said, feigning a shocked expression and sighing loudly for dramatic emphasis.

The hornet, obviously distracted by this shift in the previously benign conversation, walked boldly back and forth in front of Christina, all her faculties fully focused on the four chubby feet belonging to one wicked cow with a subtle but determined sense of humor. Despite her reservation about humans, the little hornet hopped up on my knee and stared into my face. "Do *you* see any shoes?" she asked me, nodding back in Christina's direction. But Christina, whose heart is bigger than Milwaukee, suddenly realized that her newfound friend was genuinely upset over this matter and hastened to end her distress.

"Truth is," Her Cowness began, "all shoes are really just like wings."

The little hornet and I just looked at each other and shook our heads. Christina was not to be deterred, however.

"Shoes merely represent one's own means of flight," Christina continued gently. "Symbolically speaking, of course, shoes of the mind, heart, and soul. If we ask them to, they will lift us high above all kinds of mental and emotional debris, allowing us a broader, even kinder perspective to everything in our lives—including getting one's sock muddied up or a menacing human with a can of insecticide. Furthermore, these special kinds of shoes allow us to run, dance, climb to all those places from which the imagination calls to us, from a land deep below the ocean, to the very pinnacle of the clouds. Some shoes even come with special lights, so that you can never lose your way, even in your darkest moments."

She sighed deeply at the images she was spinning for us, and then continued. "Physical shoes *visibly* worn by humans, however—

and cows, of course—are merely the out-picturing of all that is sure and wondrous and strong with the mind and heart of the wearer. They ground us and guide us; they were never meant to be weapons. And, my dear friend, when one's shoes wear out, it is time to shed old customs, habits, and thoughts and put on something new that is light, quick, and beautiful: wings, again. Without shoes, we'd never get to go cloud-dancing! You might try a pair or six some day."

The hornet seemed satisfied by Christina's poetic explanation of footgear in general. But even though she may have given a momentary thought to shodding her own multiple feet, apparently she did not feel quite prepared to do so, perhaps on some deeper, subconscious Jungian level. We could see the arguments, pro and con, seesawing in her brain, for there was considerable head shaking, reexamination of her own feet, and then more shaking of the head. At last she spoke. "I believe shoes would only be an unnecessary duplication for me since I already have wings."

"An excellent point," Christina replied.

The hornet bowed deeply. "I am off to find winter," she said. "My year is about done and it is uncommon for me to be awake at this time."

Christina returned the respectful gesture and bid her hornet friend a safe and pleasant journey. "Look for me in the clouds!" she called after the ascending insect. "I'll be the one with the new shoes!" And as the hornet disappeared from our view, my massive, mischievous companion turned back to me.

"So, she said with that deadpan expression for which cows are so famous, "want to go shopping?"

12   IT'S ALL IN THE COWSUIT

"NOT REALLY," I REPLIED. "I'M NOT MUCH OF A STORE SHOPPER. I prefer using the Internet—less crowded."

"Me, too!" Christina exclaimed, as if she had finally found her soul-sister. I thought she must be joking—again—when she continued with: "So, speaking of eBay, I just updated my PayPal account and bought this outfit. What do you think?" And she proceeded to twist her ample frame back and forth as if she were studying herself in an imaginary full-length mirror. Maybe the sun was in my eyes, or I needed more sleep, but I could see nothing different about her coat. Still auburn and white. Hereford—you know; standard issue.

"No, no, *no!*" she exclaimed, turning sharply toward me. "Can't you see? It's my power suit—just arrived yesterday. I rather fancy it, don't you?" She extended her right front foot forward in the manner of a supermodel. All she needed was a runway. Admittedly, my beloved cow sees on levels and dimensions still hidden from my own awareness. Perhaps she can even manipulate matter and energy at whim, creating whole universes on the tip of her tail and then tossing them into oblivion. Or so she's said. Still, the suit matter remained questionable. Perhaps she was overstressed because of her, er, job?

"Hardly," she scoffed, brushing off her "sleeve" with her nose. "Notice the pleats, will you? Had them specially tailored; it adds that extra *oomph* of sophistication to the whole ensemble."

Truly, her coat was beautiful—full and plush for winter, shiny and sleek. *Did I detect a zipper?*

"Suits make the cow, don't you think?" She was studying me

with that this-is-a-trick-question look. I quickly gathered my (decidedly scattered) brain cells. "I thought the inner self was what really mattered," I countered, cleverly.

"And the outer reflects the inner," she returned, deftly.

"But overemphasis on one's wardrobe," I replied sternly, "is egotistical."

"Or," Christina whispered determinedly, "a statement of one's true nature."

I scoffed dramatically, stubbornly continuing my line of thought: "... when, in fact, one then becomes merely a clotheshorse."

Christina coughed politely. "In fact, a clothes*cow*."

Touché.

Her Boldness took a last look in her "mirror" and shuffled contentedly into her house. Hay was the topic of the moment— literally. Not much room for wise words, wisecracks, or other-wise. Noon snacktime ruled. But as she turned her back to me, I thought I saw a belt buckle.

Late that evening, stars caught the elusive sun and sent bright melodies dancing all around us. This was our ritual: shared contemplative time, always sweet. As we lean against each other, we rarely speak aloud. No need to. With even our thoughts stilled, we can open to all-time, all-space, often dissolving our borders into the full and gracious universe. This evening, however, the discussion of shoes and clothes begged completion. Questions tickled my Irish temperament. Since Christina's hay supply for the day was now reduced to weedy stalks and no longer a distraction, it was time to ask about the zipper—and buckle.

"A symbolic way of opening to, or shutting out, what is rightfully ours," she said quietly, responding to my thoughts, "and that would be the sacredness that flows through all life and form. For example," she continued, "*all* you are is sacred to me. From your mind to your heart, from your shoes to your hat—all of it is important. And so, I allow you into my sphere of existence with great joy. And, may I add, you clothe your inner self magnificently." She pointed her left ear skyward. "The stars, reflecting the sun's light, are part of night's coat," she said reverently. "Clouds and rainbows—ah! The perfect accessories."

I was beginning to see her point. "Outer dressings of the soul?"

"Precisely, dear student," she replied. "What is within you will, inevitably, reflect in your wardrobe and footgear choices. And, in turn, the colors and styles you outwardly wear speak to and inwardly influence those who gaze upon you. You are, in fact, demonstrating Who You Really Are, or..." and she waited expectantly for my answer.

"My Truth?" I replied. She sighed, pleased with the lesson and my (obviously correct) answer.

I looked at the trees still turning in their autumn cycle, lit up in the moon's full light—gold, red, deep green; at the variety of branch styles, from the weeping willow to the grandiose oak, and between them, the humble, bristly Virginia pine. Indeed, didn't each form offer a glimpse of their individual personalaties, of their true nature? I thought about stones and rocks, mountains, oceans, single drops of rain. Snowflakes, flame, herbs, and flowers... seeing each one now in their "suits," glimpsing their souls. And not a one of them was trying to be something else; a tree "dressing" as a rock, or water trying to be fire.

Christina yawned. Midnight. Deep night's dark velvetness enwrapping ancient, wise, red-and-white cow-suited teacher, and sweatshirted, blue-jeaned, ever-humbled human student, in maternal comfort. I looked to Christina and "thought" my gratitude. She bowed in response, and as she did, I swear I saw buttons down her back.

13   A WEIGHTY LESSON FOR THE TEACHER

WHILE IT IS TRUE THAT I MAY AVOID SHOPPING, ESPECIALLY IN MALLS and the so-called superstores, once in a while I figure I should leave the mountains and venture out into the world, fully aware, of course, that like Cinderella I must be home by 4:00 P.M. for the evening feeding. So on the Monday after Thanksgiving I decided to start my Christmas shopping, and drove the twenty-two miles to Charlottesville.

Usually, trips off the property are made for supplies, or to one veterinary clinic or another; I really cannot travel far. Like a dedicated rubber band, I can go only a certain distance for a few hours before I have to return to my home on the hill to tend to the many creatures in my care. The old dogs, or those with chronic health or separation anxiety issues, require at least an eighteen-hour day from me, seven days a week. Planning anything long-term is wishful thinking, as I never know when one of the animals will suddenly need an emergency visit to the animal hospital. My life really does, by necessity, flow with the moment, although I can easily lose track of the positive aspect of such an existence, feeling instead that my life is out of control.

But I love my work, as a writer, a caregiver to special needs dogs and cats, especially, as well as the other animals here, and helping people through their grieving process when their own animal companion has died. Comfortably set in the foothills of the Blue Ridge Mountains, this modest place is truly a sanctuary, a "garden" that grows and nourishes all beings with equal appreciation and care. The older I grow, the more I love just being here and the less I would choose to be far away for any time at all.

This time, however, I was enticed from my routine by thoughts of brightly decorated shops and holiday music. I contemplated finding lovely gifts for my friends and family and the joy they would feel unwrapping them on Christmas morning. Happy anticipation was mine—until I reached Charlottesville and reality. The malls were overflowing with anxious people pushing and grabbing in a most un-holiday-like manner. Sales clerks were tired and cranky, and exhausted children cried and pulled at their parents.

I thought about home. The dogs and cats would all be sleeping in sunny places around the kitchen and living room. Christina would be in her upper pasture chewing cud, and the donkeys would be grazing up behind her fence. Peace... and oh yes, so quiet. I was determined to at least enjoy the Christmas decorations while I searched for those perfect gifts, and I smiled at the salespeople, thanking each one for their help. I remembered Christina's words a few weeks back, about being a light rather than a shadow as I went through my day.

But barely two hours into my adventure, I suddenly felt overwhelmed. I ached for the mountains and fresh air, but most of all, for the company of my animals. I made one final stop for coffee before heading back down Route 29 South toward my beloved Batesville. On the drive home, Christina wedged herself into my thoughts. I love that cow dearly, so the image of her broad, deadpan expression made me laugh aloud. Then, so typical of me, fear seeped in. I thought about her enormous body, a good 1,500 pounds, her veterinarian had guessed. "She has to lose the extra weight," he had warned. In fact, her enormous frame had recently become a critical issue when both back hooves developed vertical cracks. Simply put, her weight was becoming too great for her legs and feet. If she did not lose a substantial amount of poundage, within two years she would become crippled in her stifle joints, an irreparable condition. Cutting to the point: It would mean the end of her life.

So by the time I neared home I was quite out of the Christmas spirit and in complete despair. I decided, however, that it was pointless to wallow any deeper; what I needed was a plan. I recalled Christina's junk drawer and mentally devised my own. *Okay, I thought, here's my junk drawer, and I am putting my concern about Christina over here on the right.* "I have no idea how you will get the weight off of her," the vet had said. Suddenly, the imaginary drawer was overflowing with panic. No good; that left no room for the solution.

I mentally emptied the "drawer" of even my mildest concern and tried to not focus so hard on finding a solution. And suddenly, there it was—the direction I needed, just as I turned the car up the driveway and parked close to the fence where Christina now stood in front of the barn. My awesome cow eyed me suspiciously. Did she have any idea of what I was up to? She backed up four steps—one for each foot, but not so carefully that I didn't notice her mid-bulk swaying precariously from side to side. Yes, no doubt about it; we were going to get that weight off.

The next morning I showed up at the barn dressed in rather stylish sweats and at last—new sneakers purchased just the day before. Cheerful and enthusiastic, I was determined to set the tone for what was to follow. Briefly I explained to Christina what we were going to be doing every single day from now on, until she had lost at least three hundred pounds. I was confident that this was a good plan, a positive step forward. Strict diet changes would be immediately set into place, followed by aerobic exercise.

"So, are you ready?" I asked happily (feeling at last in control of at least this situation). "Here we go! *FIVE-six-seven-eight, and step, and step, and turn...*"

Halfway through my turn I looked over my shoulder at a very disgruntled cow. "I seem to be the only one exercising here," I remarked with blatant exasperation. After all, I was sweating for both of us while she stood stock-still in the cool barn. A virtual sweatband adorned her broad forehead but it gathered not a drop while my face ran like a river. Ignoring her silence, I began again. "Okay, take it from the top—five-six..." My foot paused in midair while hers remained buttoned to the ground.

"I'm not interested in silly exercises," Christina said belligerently. "I am perfectly happy with my weight, thank you; it is Who I Am." She stared down her nose in defiance and stomped her left hoof for emphasis.

Not to be discouraged, I leapt in enthusiastically with: "Yes! Again! *And step, and step, and...*" I could have continued with *turn* and found success, for my bovine friend (although she was on the verge of disowning me) had turned clear around, leaving me to look at her enormous tail-end. I walked over and tapped her on her back, but she did not respond. I tapped again. Still no response. With that, I whacked her on her hip with force equal to one good friend slapping another on the back in greeting. And with that she bent her head around to glare at me.

"You see," I said calmly, "you have so much weight here, you didn't even feel me touch you gently on the back. So, it takes a good slugging to get your attention!" She wasn't laughing. But I wasn't either. This was serious business.

Christina, however, saw things differently. At the present moment (and here she would point out, *Do we really have anything else?*), she felt fit and fine, albeit lurching like a ship on a stormy sea as she walked, but nothing a mind-over-matter attitude couldn't fix. And then there were the meals of sweet feed: oats, corn, and molasses—the high point of her days, always anticipated with great excitement, and later, happily recalled while it all digested in four stomach chambers for several blissful hours.

But now, Rita, her irreverent (in her eyes) so-called friend-turned-nemesis, was changing everything. Suddenly the grain was gone from her food dish, replaced with a strange mix of mineral supplement and garlic. Ugh. And her hay ration? Pitiful! The great arm loads she was used to had become a piddling mouthful, suitable in quantity for a mouse, perhaps (if they ate hay, that is). And now, exercise. All Christina heard was "Walk, Christina; get up and get moving, Christina; run, Christina!" And the most humiliating? Something about *step and step and turn*?

Torture, mortification, doom, the end of the eternal picnic. Could a cow's life get any worse?

"Decidedly," I said quietly, steadily, trying to keep the panic out of my voice. But she knew; blessed cow was once again reading my thoughts.

"I am not interested in putting you down simply because you got too fat," I said.

"But maybe it would be my time," she countered. "I might as well go out happy." I thought I heard her stomach gurgling.

"NO!" I cried. "This is a stupid argument! Look at me; I was getting a bit hefty, decided it was not a healthy direction, and I have lost eight pounds in six weeks. I feel much better, and so will you."

Tepid eyes studied me from head to foot. "Puny," was all she said.

"I beg your pardon?"

"I said, you're puny. Why would I want to emulate that?" She was obviously not going to budge on the subject. Nor could she. She appeared to be wedged between the stall walls. There was a slight grunt, then a sigh.

"Could you possibly come 'round in front of me and give me a push backwards?" She asked in a quite subdued tone of voice.

I studied the awkward situation, realized with her being bodily stuck as she was, the situation was screaming for an *I told you so*. But I didn't press it. Kindness swept over me, compassion dug in, and relief at the thought of possibly changing her stubborn attitude swelled my brain with endorphins. "Sure," I replied nonchalantly. "Glad to help a friend in distress." (I probably put a bit more emphasis on *distress* than was necessary.)

I had to crawl under her to get to her head, then flatten myself against the front of the stall just to face her, and I did so graciously, without complaint. But I could tell she was a bit embarrassed, for when I suggested that she try and suck in her sides and she couldn't, the inside of her ears became a flaming pink.

"Right, then," I said cheerfully, "breathe in on the count of three and heave back as I push, otherwise you might be here till next Wednesday."

Placing my hands flat on her all-but-nonexistent shoulders, I began to count. When I reached three, I heard an enormous intake of air, much like a pipe organ dying, and I began to push as hard as I could. There was a squeaking sound as the mass of hungry cow lurched backward and out of the stall. The whole scenario reminded me of her once getting jammed in the door of the feed shed and how she had nearly dismembered the entire front of the barn in the process of freeing herself. Yes, the time had come for my strict weight-reduction program.

My wise and wonderful friend, realizing that sometimes the teacher also needs to learn, humbled herself by adjusting her virtual sweatband higher on her forehead, extending one front hoof, and beginning in a resigned yet steady voice: "Five, six, seven, eight—and step, and step, and turn, oh my!" And she executed a perfect turn. When she had realigned herself to face me, she bowed her head and said simply, "Thank you."

"Sure," I replied. "No sweat."

All together now—five, six, seven, eight, and step, and step, and turn…

14 STILL LIFE WITH CLUTTER

You know how it is—once Thanksgiving has gone by, the December holidays loom large and fast. As one who celebrates Christmas, over the years I have traditionally joined the untold numbers of frantic souls who are suddenly faced with card sending, gift buying, home decorating, and baking the requisite piles of cookies, cakes, and cranberry breads—all at the same time. *But not this year.* Through Christina's careful lessons I was finally beginning to honor the priorities in all aspects of my life. And bowing to the "obligations" of a commercialized Christmas was off my holiday list. That one shopping foray into Charlottesville had reminded me that December twenty-fifth should not be a deadline to meet, but a pinnacle of peace, joy, love, and reverence, to emulate and share with the world, moment by moment, no matter what the day, or month. So, standing in the middle of my as-yet-undecorated (except for a new wreath) living room, I announced to the dogs, cats, and non- hibernating ladybugs that I was committing my time and effort toward a more spiritual approach to the season. Even though my audience seemed unimpressed, I was so pleased with myself that I decided to share my decision with Christina.

Out in the barn, the early December wind whipped through the open doors and ample cracks. I pulled my heavy farm jacket around me and strode purposefully into Christina's stall to face her back end, swaying back and forth. Unintelligible mumbling burbled from a pile of fresh hay, a broad pink bovine nose buried deep into its midst. Christina stomped her front feet—first the left, then the right, her traditional response when agitated. Bits of hay flew everywhere; I saw no sign of the usual careful selection, rolling stems about the mouth, lengthy chewing, slide-down-the-throat, and so forth. This action was definitely different. Tentatively, I tapped her on her back, just above her tail. Her head flew up and out, and hay scattered everywhere.

"I'm looking for something," she said, obviously frustrated. "I know I put it in here somewhere... When will I ever learn to keep this closet clean..." And her head disappeared into the hay pile once again.

Closet? Oh, my beloved cow. A pile of hay is a pile of hay; put it there myself at eight-thirty this morning, wishing her a pleasant breakfast and a joyous day. But with the world situation being bleak and sliding fast, I decided the whole closet issue was very small. I could let it go and stay with the current program. Hers, of course. And I was feeling in a useful mood, so I asked, "What are you looking for? Maybe I can help you find it."

Out popped her head again, eyes wide, the small fluff of rust-colored hair atop her head, disheveled.

"A book of Zen poetry, one of my favorites. Can't imagine where it went to. I had put it on that upper shelf, but with all the other stuff in there..."

I leapt clean over the shelf reference to ask, "*Stuff?*"

"Oh, you know, the usual. Everyone has a closet full of stuff. The kind of closet you can't open the door to because everything falls out on your head."

"You're not being specific," I replied. "I can't help you find the book if you don't tell me what I'm *not* looking for."

"Come again?" she said tersely.

I continued, undeterred. "I said, I need to know what all the stuff is, so I know it is not your book. Then, when I see a book that doesn't look anything like—"

At this point, I thought I heard her growl, but I could have been mistaken. Her eyelids dropped in all-consuming exasperation so unlike her.

"Dear one," she started slowly, "I am not feeling very centered at the moment. Please excuse me. I wanted to spend some quiet time with my favorite poet, but what I have encountered is an enormous obstacle."

I could have said, "A closet that isn't really there? A shelf that rests high in your imagination?" But I knew she had already read my thoughts, browsed through my thought-forms, and had, miraculously, chosen to ignore them. I would play along. "And that would be?" I asked.

"Clutter. Endless clutter. Will I ever stop collecting stuff I no longer need, let alone want? Look at this closet! Can't even see the shelves or the floor." She pushed at something with her front left hoof. "Now why am I hanging onto this tennis racket?"

"Because you don't know how to play tennis yet, and you'd like to learn?" I ventured cautiously. Again, I got the stern and narrowed gaze.

"I played professional tournaments for three years, thank you very much. But I've moved on to other things. You know, one does grow into new directions and interests."

"So what's your new direction now?" I was trying to visualize her in tennis whites; the shorts were a stretch, even for my writer's mind.

Christina was looking distant—not in an unfriendly manner, but more the right-brain-dominant artist or poet drifting on clouds of inspiration.

"Watercolor painting, for one," she sighed. "And poetry. Zen is especially appealing for its simplicity. I have thought of combining these two media of creative expression; what do you think?"

I looked around for an easel; didn't see one, of course. She cleared her throat, tipping her head upward in small, repeated bobs. Eventually, I recognized the signal and looked up. It was absolutely astonishing. While the ceiling of the barn appeared to be just that—the ceiling of the barn, cobwebs and all—there was yet an unmistakable sense of something else. I closed my eyes and defocused my brain. When I looked up again, I saw paintings! Dozens of them. Watercolor renderings of sky and clouds, mountains and meadows; birds in rows on a pasture fence; the sea at high tide; cows sitting, cows dancing, cows in orchestras, cows—yup, playing tennis. It was all too wonderful to doubt. The paintings ranged from those that were large and carefully framed, to minuscule and raggedy-edged sheets of sketchbook paper. It was a feast. I blinked, only to find, once again, a blank barn ceiling.

"Oh, my," I whispered in awe.

"And you should see my sketchbook!" Christina exclaimed, obviously delighted I was able to "see" her work. She was quite proud.

And so was I. Of her, of course, for she obviously displayed incredible artistic ability. But I was also proud of myself, for being able to see on an alternate level. Was I actually maturing spiritually? Naturally, I returned from my self-indulgent musings to find my sweet cow studying me without expression. Translated into Bovinese, this meant: *At last my student is doing her homework.* There would be more to all of this, I knew. And here it came.

"Tell me about my closet," she said quietly. "What could it represent, relative to your own life?"

Oh, too easy. "My frantic mind; my overfull life." I replied.

"Good," she said without emotion. "Wouldn't you say this could apply to just about all the humans you know?"

"But you have a closet, and you're a—"

"Cow? I would hope so. But also, your teacher. I get to manifest what I need to help you see—"

"See *through* the clutter!" I was catching on.

"Precisely. And when you do, what will you find?"

I don't know why I said it, but: "One beautiful thing."

"Bingo!"

"So," she continued, settling into a comfortable position, "what is your next step? What do you practice *seeing* next?"

"Your closet?"

"Yup. Give it a shot."

Well, first I had to believe there actually was a closet, real or figurative, in all that hay. And I didn't, not completely. And that 1.2 percent of disbelief was enough to keep me from seeing on Christina's more-expanded level. But I was willing to give it a try. To get in the mood, I once again I looked up at the barn ceiling, physically seeing hundred-year-old wooden boards and defunct spiderwebs. While those were also interesting, that Something Else was again nudging my consciousness. So I closed my eyes, defocused my brain, and voilà! Still lifes and landscapes, cow portraits and—wait a minute—one of me!

There was a polite hiccup beside me. "You're getting off track," she said.

Nodding (with one more admiring glance at my likeness on the ceiling), I dialed my focus to "blank"—really; completely, non-judging *blank*. And there it was, the most stylish armoire you have ever seen. "That's hardly a mere closet," I remarked. "Where on Earth did you find it?"

Christina smiled. "Oh, not on Earth. But that's not the point here." There was a short huffing sound beside me.

"Okay," I said. "What now?" I was still immersed in the blankness—punctuated by the ornate armoire—in my mind.

"Open the doors," Christina whispered. "But stand back when you do." She began to sound agitated again.

In my mind I carefully reached for the two round wooden handles and pulled on them very slowly. Out poured the most amazing collection of... stuff that any cow could hope to stash in an entire garage, let alone a cow closet. And then, all the "stuff" in my mind, too! But as it all fell around me, it seemed to dissolve, to turn into fine mist and blow away. And in the end I was left sitting on the barn floor, hay in my ears and down my jacket, the open doors of the armoire showing nothing more than a series of—you guessed it—shelves.

And One Absolutely Beautiful Thing: a book, bound in burgundy-colored cloth, edged in shimmering gold. My mind's hand reached in and carefully picked it up. And then, on impulse, I opened my eyes. The armoire was not there; only the original pile of hay. But in my hand lay that single book.

"You found it!" Christina exclaimed. "Bless your heart. You found my book of Zen poetry. Will you stay a while and read some of it to me?"

So we settled down into the magical pile of hay, I against her broad, warm side, reading exquisite poetry aloud, and she listening happily, eyes closed in bliss, to her favorite volume, as worlds and dimensions whirled and interblended around us, like the most brilliant of watercolor paintings.

15   DONE IT SO LONG

I STAYED A LONG TIME DEEP IN THAT HAY, READING TO CHRISTINA from her most precious possession. After a while she stared out into the December day, her eyes glazed as she absorbed the words and images flowing around her. And then she closed her eyes again, taking long deep breaths, as if drawing in those words through all the pores of her body, her head beginning to drop as she moved into a deep and peaceful sleep.

I laid the little book beside her and tiptoed from the barn so as not to wake her. A misting rain was beginning to fall as the temperatures moved up with a shifting southerly airflow. It would have all felt surreal and un-Christmas-like except for the light and peace that still enveloped me. I recalled why I had gone out to the barn that morning in the first place, and realized I no longer felt the need to talk about my newfound priorities, even to Christina. Being peace, being the poetry we had just shared, was "conversation" enough.

Back inside the house I checked on two of my oldest creatures, both of whom had cancer but seemed stable and happy. Fifteen-year-old Sophie, my wheaten-colored, midsized terrier, was sleeping comfortably on her dog bed, while Cleo, my somewhat feisty and strong-willed sixteen-year-old white cat, was in my office, curled up in her box by her favorite window. I felt a familiar weariness move through me as I watched them, knowing their time with me was short. I dreaded their leaving, dreaded the grieving I knew I had to pass through. And at Christmas time, no less.

Christmas: a way of being; a pinnacle of peace, joy, love, and reverence...to share moment by moment.... My own determination echoed around my mind and I breathed out. It was, after all, obviously not yet the time to grieve for my two little friends.

Now, approaching afternoon feeding time, I decided to go back outside and start the hour-long process, beginning with cleaning and refilling the water buckets. But as I reached the donkeys' bucket, a small movement in the water caught my attention.

I reached my hand down and a tiny insect, apparently stirred earlier from winter sleep by the warm, moist air, reached up toward my finger. Without hesitation she clung tightly as I lifted her from the water. Her wings, so fragile and brilliantly luminescent, lay flattened down against her body. What more could I, with clumsy hands, do for someone so delicate?

"Ask the sun to help."

The deep voice from behind startled me, nearly causing me to drop my soggy friend. The voice, now embodied, strode from behind the maple tree, swinging wide her white-tipped tail. The whole cow, from head to tail, moved closer, hovered over my shoulder, breathing most carefully so as not to disturb the creature now lying prone upon my fingertip.

"She's in shock, but the sun will dry her wings and warm her," Christina continued, having emerged from her slumber apparently unaware of the dense overcast and light rain still falling on us. And with these words my beloved, if misguided, cow looked skyward, closed her eyes, and began mumbling something about *If you would be so kind... just for a minute or two... small insect... Rita... thank you.* And suddenly, a warm radiance poured around us like a holy blanket.

The tiny creature began to stir. She lifted her wings and stepped forward on nearly invisible feet. Then she was gone, rising effortlessly on soft air currents into her regained freedom.

"You did a good thing," Christina said, watching the insect disappear into the bare branches of the maple tree. "Most humans wouldn't have even noticed her in the water, let alone taken the time to help her." Then, as if to deflate any ego boost her words might have given me, she quickly added, eyes right on mine, "You've had good teachers."

"Yes," I agreed. "And you top the list."

Christina blushed (if cows can do such a thing) and shuffled her feet.

"But also," I added, "loving everyone in nature is all I know how to do. I guess I've done it for so long."

"Very noble of you," Christina said. There was a tone to her voice that put me on alert. And then she added, "Ever regret being this way?"

As a rule, cows don't voluntarily walk up to a human and demand to be adopted. Remember, if you will, how she got here—brazenly appearing and expecting to stay. There are risks: being made into future burgers, for instance, or handbags. Would the potential human view said cow in terms of market value, or as a family member? Would concern be focused on price per pound, or quality of life? So many issues to be considered before choosing which driveway to wander up in search of potential bovine-human bonding.

But that is precisely what Christina did that one winter's morning. Was this the unconscious act of a headstrong, curious calf, or the well-planned, divinely guided, this-is-the-day resolve of an ancient and wise teacher? The old saying goes like this: When the student is ready, the teacher will appear. So it would have seemed on that cold January day so many years before.

And the student, struggling with issues of her own, was definitely ready. But to my mind, there is a moral obligation in receiving one's teacher, whatever form that teacher may arrive in. The student must be willing to face the challenges the best teacher offers and graciously accept them, tough though those challenges may be.

And Christina (aka, Teacher in a Cow Suit) has always known how to stir the waters of my soul. But I have found that while, initially, said stirring results in mud, clarity is bound to be the end result. Such a challenge only makes me look deeper into myself, to help me find *Self*, within. Call it what you will, that "Self," as I see it, is composed of the purest love and the purest peace. And Christina, so obviously aware of this on both a theoretical and a practical level, already knew my answer to her question, *Ever regret being this way?* But she waited patiently for me to plunge through the inevitable "mud." With great care, she selected a soft spot on the damp brown grass and settled in.

I, in no hurry to answer, wept. Her question had, indeed, opened Pandora's Box. All those issues—pain for other people's insensitivity; all the good-byes to beloved friends who were changing worlds; all the senselessness, cruelty, neglect, abandonment—all of these emotions were rushing and jostling through my brain. The agony of memory stung, and stung again.

Christina laid her broad chin, light as a leaf, across my shoulder. A tear dropped from each of her enormous brown eyes—tears for *my* tears.

"My sorrow," she said softly, confirming my thoughts, "comes from the fact that you still can't see the Greater Truth (note the Capital 'T', please). That is why I came here—to help you recognize and live fully as that Greater Truth, and to recognize how that Greater Truth combines and flows together with your own truth."

"And that is?"

"That among other things, nothing about life and living needs to be so hard!" she replied, leaning back.

"I don't understand," I said.

"The Truth I want to help you find," she began, "is found, yes, in nature all around you, but also within *you*. Your own place of Truth assures you that where there is hurt, there is also the potential for forgiveness. Where there is pain, there is the opportunity for healing. And where there is darkness, there is also always Light. Capital 'L' please. When you instinctively extended your hand and heart to that little insect, you were, through your intention to help another struggling being, reaching from that point of Truth, or Love and Peace within yourself. Your intention motivated your action to help her past the darkness of her own struggle and fear, and thus encouraged her to trust the love you were extending to her. Done unconditionally and with humility, such an action becomes a blessing that has no boundaries. It becomes the unveiling of the Greater Truth of a perfection of Love that is always present."

Not sure why, suddenly I remembered the little dog, Oliver, who had come into my care several years ago. He had been covered in cigarette burns, among other atrocities imposed on his innocent self. Now anger and grief spread like a wildfire through my brain, displacing any thoughts of Love, Peace, or Truth.

Christina studied my face, my hands clenched into fists, my drawn-down shoulders.

"Oliver forgave those who abused him. He purposefully came to you to teach you forgiveness. Do you remember what a joyful little dog he was? That, my dear, was his True Nature, his unbounded soul revealed to you the entire time you were together. Can you honor him by following his example?"

Christina's challenge was intensifying. But I knew she was right.

I sighed, settling in the grass beside her. It occurred to me that chewing cud might calm my nerves. "I guess I've also done fear and grief and anger for so long, as well as caregiving and compassion and love, that at times, *these* are all I know how to do. I'm not very proud of myself."

But Christina was unconcerned with my self-pity. She tucked her right foot under her. "No; you should be glad for who you are. You, like everyone else, are Soul: searching, learning, expanding, experiencing, adventuring... in a life and a world that rises to all your expectations and responds in kind to your every thought. If you will just turn and look with your heart, you will see that there is no end to the wonder in everything. So just continue to reach out with your heart, share what you know to be Truth (Capital 'T', please), be grateful for everything, and have no regrets. Oliver didn't."

My teacher closed her eyes and began to snore softly. The sun reached down and outward, pushing away the last of the dampness as my tiny insect friend alighted on the fence rail next to me and bowed her Thanks, with a capital "T." And I realized my answer to Christina's question was simply this: *No, I have never had any regrets being this way.*

16   HERE AND EVERYWHERE

SOPHIE'S SPIRIT WALKED ACROSS THE RAINBOW BRIDGE FIVE DAYS later; Cleo's followed the next week. I felt as if I had been smashed with a fierce one-two knockout punch that sent me sprawling facedown onto the proverbial "mat" of inner and outer peace. So much of my own belief system reassured me that both my friends were now happily free of old, ill bodies. And, I felt honored and glad to have been so much a part of their last years on Earth. Yet my ever-so-human self grieved, and I wept long and hard, missing them more than I could bear.

All my past experiences with animals and human friends (including my mother) who had died, reminded me that I would survive these losses as well. I would eventually move past the pain, opening my home to new creatures and my heart to new friends. This became my beacon as I made my way through the first, toughest days following Sophie's and Cleo's deaths.

But now it was Christmas Eve, and all I could focus on were my two old friends, buried out in the yard. I was hardly what one would call "in the holiday spirit." By 11:00 P.M., while the rest of my human and creature family slept, I was staring at the living room wall, tears pouring down on either side of my snuffly nose. While it was an odd time to visit Christina, my grief was enormous, and I was desperate for her wise words and warm companionship.

Outside, stars—my dazzling companions, constant and sincere—spread above me in a domed and new-moon sky. Tiptoeing into the barn, I found my beloved cow deep in a bed of clean hay, her head turned back on her shoulder but not yet asleep. For a long time we said nothing. Christina dozed, woke to chew cud, dozed again. I studied the mountains, two-dimensional in their blackness, appropriate for my mood.

"I miss them so much," I whispered to the stars.

"Me, too," my sleepy cow said, her eyes now closed.

"What do you mean, 'Me, too'? You never met them."

"Cows know everyone in and out of physical body."

Christina opened her eyes and studied the hay in front of her. "And I liked them a lot, especially that crusty old cat."

"When?" I asked.

"When what?"

"When did you meet Cleo?"

"Yesterday."

"That's not possible," I exclaimed. "She died two days ago."

"Physically, yes," Christina replied with a deep sigh. "Cleo her *Self*," she continued, "dropped by to visit with me yesterday afternoon."

"Why didn't you tell me sooner?" Surely she knew how sad I was.

She swung her enormous head to focus directly on my eyes. "Because you didn't ask me," she said. "It is not my nature to intrude."

I had nothing to say for quite a while. I felt ashamed for my outburst, but the more I looked into her eyes, the more compassion I felt pouring from them. Not only would she not intrude, I felt assured that she would accept and love me in all my ways and temperaments.

"Oh," was all I could manage. And then I dropped my gaze. Christina shifted in her well-packed bedding and stuck one short, chubby leg out in front of her.

" 'O' is correct," she said brightly. "Since you bring up the subject of circles, may I remind you about them? And have I told you about the Garden yet?"

"No," I replied.

"The Garden exists everywhere—on all planes, crossing through, in, and out of time and space. It is completely limitless and very, very beautiful. And because the Garden is without limitations, it exists here as well as in what you call 'The Other Side.' Both Sophie and Cleo are simply in that aspect of the Garden that vibrates at a higher energy pulsation than what most humans are aware of. But both Sophie and Cleo, and countless others you have known, are here, nonetheless. Neither has actually left or gone away. They are just Everywhere, and by its very definition, Everywhere must also be here. It's really very simple." And she turned her head back onto her shoulder again and closed her eyes. A large and frosty sigh rose from her nose.

I pulled my thick jacket around me and leaned into her for warmth. Now totally confused by her words, I decided to take her often-stated advice to *Always ask if you don't understand.*

"I don't understand," I said flatly. "What on Earth are you talking about?"

Christina swung her head back around to face front. "What—on Earth—is correct. Now ask yourself, 'What—beyond the visible world'—and you will have your answer." But her words were still not making sense to me.

"Look in the sky," she said softly. "What do you see?"

"Stars," I replied.

"And why are you able to see those stars?"

"Because they are reflecting the sun's light?"

"Precisely," she said. "But where is the sun? Can you see it right now?"

"Of course not!" I laughed. "It's nearly midnight. The sun is around the other side of the Earth."

"Bingo. You can't see the sun, but it's always out there, and you know it. In case you do forget, in the rush of things, the stars are there to remind you that the sun is not 'gone' or 'dead' or 'lost.' It's just on the other side—physically speaking—of the planet, and out of view." She turned and looked at me. "It's the same when someone dies, or steps out of their physical body. They are on the other side. You can't see them, but they still exist. And just to remind you, their spirit-light reflects off of everything you can still see and feel and sometimes even hear, like a brush against your cheek, or a song on the radio that suddenly seems to be a message from someone who has died."

I was really confused now. "But what does that have to do with a garden?"

"Not just a garden, my dear, but *the* Garden, where everything moves in rhythms and pulses and waves and cycles," Christina replied. "Whether it is the Earth moving around the sun, time moving through the cycles of seasons, day into night into day again—Soul moving into body, out of body into spirit form, back into body again."

She rose from her nest of warm hay, stretched, and took two steps out of the barn to look around in the soft night. "The garden I speak of," she said, "represents all of life here on Earth and everywhere—places and dimensions and vibrational levels your scientists are only just beginning to discover. But science aside, for ease of reference, mystics and all of nature—including cows—refer to it all simply as the Garden. Think of it in this way: Go out into your own garden at various times of the year. During some seasons, there will be new physical growth, and in other times, very developed growth with flowers and fruit. Then there comes a time when the garden dies back, goes to ground for a while. But during this time, even during all seasons, the reawakening and the potential for new growth waits, fully alive, for its perfect time to return."

"And that's where Sophie and Cleo are? And all my other friends who have died?"

She nodded, shaking the cold off her russet coat. I rose from the hay and turned toward the house, a familiar trek for a weary spiritual student.

"I have just one more question," I said, stopping short of the gate and turning back. "If you are able to see and hear Sophie and Cleo since they died, why did you say you miss them?"

Christina looked so kindly at me, like a compassionate mother would look before wrapping comforting arms around her forlorn child. "Because, my dear friend," she said, "when the physical form that is so soft to touch, so beautiful to look upon, so wonderful to be near, falls away, yes, there is a definite kind of loss, and your sorrow for that loss is absolutely valid. That is what I miss as well... Sophie playing out in the yard with you, Cleo sitting up in her window, watching the birds. Lovely. I miss that part of them. I am, after all, still a Cow!"

"Oh," I said quietly. I looked one more time at the stars and returned to the house, thinking about gardens.

Dawn had not even entered the picture when I woke from a deep and confused sleep. My first thought of the day was simply, *It's Christmas, and Cleo and Sophie are gone.* I lay in the dark and considered everything Christina had told me in the middle of the night, realizing I still had just too many questions on such an important subject as where those friends of mine go when they die.

I waited to ask those questions until an hour decent for cattle: after breakfast, just before morning nap, when cud-chewing is well under way but not yet too involved. Trying to appear upbeat, I popped around the corner of Christina's stall, startling her.

"Merry Christmas!" I exclaimed encircling my arms around her neck.

"Oh, it's you," she remarked, as she resettled into her routine.

"And you were expecting someone else?" I asked.

"Not at all," she replied. "I was just speaking with Sophie, and now I've lost track of what I was saying, but never mind—it's always good to see you." She fell into that irritating way of abruptly ending our conversation by extending out her head, laying back her ears just so, and setting her eyes into a vacant half-stare. She was as absent as one can be and still be in-body.

I, of course, was stunned, crammed with questions, and rapidly descending into overwrought, hypertensive anxiety. This was no time for chewing cud, absolutely the wrong occasion for a nap. I simply could not let Her Cowship get away with this one more time.

"What do you mean, you were 'speaking with Sophie'?"

Christina sighed, a burble escaping from deep in her chest. A wad of cud floated effortlessly up her throat and found its place on her ample molars. "Sophie was telling me how she had to rest for a while after she left her body. Her death was not an easy one, as you know. But she's feeling much better now in her spirit self and will be here for as long as you need her. She's formless, of course, but ready to resume her appointed duties." Christina never stopped chewing as she spoke, her words slow and drawn out, bovine fashion. "Understand now?"

No, I didn't. I didn't understand any of it, but I was undeterred. So while Christina began her morning rounds of checking water buckets, nibbling from various piles of hay, and depositing manure in discreet areas of her field, I was right behind her, questions pouring out of my overloaded brain like water rushing from a downspout.

"I agree that death is a large subject, but you can't argue with dying," she said offhandedly.

"I don't follow," I replied, two steps behind her. "Your species fights the process. Death is important, a good thing in its own time—just another step outward, if you will, in a boundless Life,

Capital 'L.' " She stopped to admire a cardinal in a pine tree. "Consider," she continued, "that animals, including Sophie and Cleo and that bird up there, already know about the Garden, where everything is possible and there are no limitations, including communicating with those no longer in physical bodies. If you will trust your intuition and what your heart tells you, then you will be able to converse across dimensions as well."

Christina turned to me and bowed her head slightly. "Not to worry; you're well on your way to achieving this ability," she said quietly. "It's a gift you will receive after much practice, and give away many times in the years ahead to others who question and grieve. After all, isn't it always Christmas?"

And then it started to snow. It would be a beautiful day after all.

17 DE-FENCED

ON THIS SIDE OF THAT MYSTERIOUS GARDEN THE LAST BRAVE violet of December had succumbed without fuss to the New Year's Day ice storm. I, on the other hand, regarded the current extreme weather conditions with concern. Gingerly crossing the slippery grass with Christina's first snack of hay, I thought for a brief, irrational moment that I saw the tip of a cow's ear poking out from the boxwood bush. "Couldn't be," I muttered to my frozen feet. "Ground's smooth as glass; she'd never make it from the barn to there." Because I had seen that ear-to-bush so many times over the past two years, I figured I must be hallucinating. It sure was cold enough to provoke such a mental state.

But the nose—that broad, pale pink, and very chilled nose protruding from the branches was all too present. No speculation here; my dear cow was firmly entrenched in said shrubbery.

As if she really wanted to be there. *No. Not. Never again.* Four pointed words that she broadcast across the ice with thoughts that prickled, bristled, and shrieked at me. Situation was this: apparently, by slipping and sliding, she had managed to follow her usual twice-daily (breakfast and dinner time) trek to the fence by the back door, positioning herself just so, to be ready when I would eventually emerge to feed her. Her knowledge and understanding of "slick as a whistle" was nil, this being her first serious ice storm. As she watched me place the hay in a pile by the fence, she took a tentative step around the bush, only to have her left hind leg skitter precariously out from under her. As she caught her balance, an unaccustomed look of distress crossed the face of the Queen of Calm.

I couldn't resist. "Get a grip, will you?" I hollered back at her over my shoulder. Then I, too, took hesitant steps toward the barn, only to spin sideways and crash shoulder first into the wall. The look on my face would have been predictable.

No doubt she would have laughed if she had been paying attention. But at the precise moment when I made contact with the wall, Christina made contact with her snack, having once again fully focused on the project at hand. And she was not to be disturbed. Perhaps her four stomach chambers sang of mealtime, but I suspected she was trying to regain her composure and figure out what to do next: sled into the stall on four chubby hooves to get the rest of her morning's hay? A reasonable idea, but not so easily accomplished considering her now-mounting, ever-more-distressing experience on the frosty stuff.

She took an incredibly long time with her snack. What would normally have been a one-minute inhalation stretched to three, four, approaching (could it be?) *five minutes* with the nose not once coming up for air. Yet that first small bunch of hay was long gone. Out of compassion I unstuck myself from the side of the barn and, inching my way along the gate, reached her broad and ruddy side. Embracing her neck, I congratulated her on her brave trek across such new territory, assuring her that the remainder of her fresh hay lay piled up for her but a few cow-lengths ahead. "Nothing to it!" I casually tossed at her; "Just follow me."

I think we would have been in clover, as the saying goes, had I not taken three steps and, with all the grace of a fire engine careening around a street corner, fallen flat on my backside. I waited for the inevitable bovine humor, a remark that would not be cruel, only quite pointed regarding human bumbling.

But there was not a peep. Turning to see if she were still in-body, the sight before me (although from my vantage point she appeared to be upside down) caused me to laugh aloud, despite the pain running up my back. There she stood, two steps behind me, one foot forward, her face (not to mention the 1,400, plus or minus, pounds of cow) frozen into a position that clearly stated she had no intention of moving until spring, or at least until the traditional January thaw. No sir, this cow would not make such a fool of herself as I had.

I righted myself, brushed away the ice chips from my jeans, and felt for broken bones. None found, I slid one foot in front of the other until I had reached the hay room and was able to backtrack, laying down a path of fresh hay for her to walk on. After several trips back and forth without further damaging myself, I was able to convince her to at last take the plunge (but not literally, of course)—to take destiny in her own hooves and bravely shuttle her enormous and quivering form into the barn. Destination achieved, we both settled down in the warm hay to discuss a matter of vast concern to me.

"Do you ever feel trapped?" I asked, shaking ice out of my boots. Christina swung her head in my direction and eyed me intensely.

"And you are asking me because... ?"

"I just wanted to know," I said. "Now, do you ever feel trapped?"

Christina never blinked. "As in 'fenced in'?"

Obviously she was thawing out nicely. Before I could reply she blinked once, then added, "No."

Humans, you know, have to belabor a point, and not wanting to break with tradition, I pushed bravely on. "I mean, when you see the cows across the road and you raise your nose and bellow at them, are you, by doing so, regretting being here by yourself rather than with them?"

Christina sighed. "I suppose I might be tempted to say yes. However, the truth is, there is really nothing in my life that is grounds for regret."

Now it was my turn to sigh. "That must be a wonderful feeling," I said, regretfully. Christina laughed. "You see, the thing is," she replied, pushing a chunk of ice from between her toes, "we cattle have learned that the happiest, healthiest moment is the present one, not what happened yesterday or an hour ago—not even what might be joyfully anticipated in the future. Looking forward to mealtime is the one exception. Beyond that, cancel expectation; just give us a now. One might rewrite the famous line, 'How Now Brown Cow' to read, 'Now, Now, is Good Enough for the Brown Cow (and all others).' It's a rough translation, you understand."

I didn't, but drove on with my questions. "Don't you have visions, dreams, plans?" I asked.

"Oh, I have a plan, everyone does, but it isn't based on dissatisfaction. And it has nothing to do with the grass being greener..."

The meager January sun had disappeared again and a new haze of snow was crossing the mountains. Falling on top of the layer of ice already on the ground, the snow would certainly make travel even more difficult. I thought about needing to get to town later and fretted over having to postpone the trip. How would I get my supplies and go to the bank and—and—and... I was aware of an incredible wave of silence from a certain cow enveloping me. The interior of my head, still wanting to rant, became very quiet.

"O-kay," I said, exhaling steadily. "Got the point." I heard Christina rotate her jaws just once, indicating that she was pleased her student had figured this one out on her own. Nonetheless, in the next second, as the snow reached where we sat and blew into my face, I began to ponder the possibility of having to shovel the stuff later in the afternoon; the weather report had called for several inches. I might not be getting out for several days if the roads didn't melt quickly enough. I would need to ration feed a bit. Why had I not for seen the storm and laid in more supplies? And—and—and...

A shift in bovine body weight brought me instantly back to the present and the realization I had a long way yet to travel to reach enlightenment. Christina just looked at me with those half-closed eyes, her jaws rotating rhythmically across wads of pulverized material.

"So how did *you* get so enlightened?" I asked.

As the current wad slipped down her throat, she replied, "I told you, I have a plan."

"And that is?"

She rolled right over my question to add, "But one not based on expectation, time, or space considerations, or dependent upon another's choices."

"Of course, but the plan is—" I said, breaking in.

She ignored my question and said, "And therefore, fences are of no concern to me."

I was convinced by now that either a) she was never going to get around to explaining precisely what her plan was, or b) she was faking it, and didn't have a plan at all. Checking my appetite, I realized I needed an early lunch and made an obvious motion to leave. Still, she did not react, but continued to expound on her plan, whatever it was. While she seemed totally absorbed in her monologue, I had by now lost all interest, my thoughts having leapt expectantly to a cup of hot chocolate and a grilled cheese sandwich.

Snow swirled around the barn as I stepped out the door, but my thoughts had beaten me to the house. In short, I neither noticed the snow nor the patch of ice, and once again landed on my backside not a foot from Christina's face. She was just winding up her explanation with: "... and so the only way to accomplish that, is *through* the wall."

I managed to scoot my hands and knees under me and with great care—and embarrassment—crawl back into the stall. Lunch seemed dismally out of reach. A warm nose poked tentatively at my shoulder. "You all right?" the words rode into my ear on cow breath laced with garlic and genuine concern.

"Sure, thanks," I said as offhandedly as I could. I was not about to admit to being mindless, much less now bruised in more places than I cared to count. Though I knew Christina could see straight through my bluff, her kindheartedness kept her from belittling me.

"*What* wall was that again?" I asked, as if I had been paying attention all along.

"Oh, the one pertinent to my plan, of course," she replied. Period. Nothing followed. I knew even less than I had at the onset of this conversation, much less whether or not she truly felt confined. But I knew that at the moment, *I* certainly did.

While I adjusted my body for all the mounting sore spots, I felt those "brown cow" eyes now studying me with unnerving calm, the sort a meditation teacher might employ while waiting for his or her student to "smarten up," so to speak.

"Had I as much expectation for the future or regret over the past as do you," she said softly, "to answer your question, yes, I would feel quite confined. The cows across the road, the pasture beyond the fence, the hay in the fields—all would be out of reach, *and should I choose to feel deprived* of any of these, I would be, most definitely, kept from that which I really desire, being happiness and peace. But you see, it would be a choice only I could make for myself. Therefore, I have chosen otherwise."

"But the wall?" I asked impatiently. I was getting tired now; I just wanted the point of the whole story.

Christina, however, was in no hurry. "Don't you see?" she continued. "When you always want something more, something just ahead, or what might have been but never was, you're always building a wall around yourself, made out of expectations and regrets. Your vision is clipped, your path is blocked; you miss all that the present moment offers. The only way out of such a mess is to have a plan that gets you through that wall."

"Oh, *that* kind of wall!" I replied with a sigh. Now she was making more sense, or perhaps I was paying better attention? "And your plan to do so is... ?" I asked.

"A few moments ago," Christina said, "getting from the bush to my hay and from there to where I am now without mishap, took tremendous concentration and careful attention. But it also called for moving with, or better yet, *as* the moment. Had I lost that concentration and carelessly taken the wrong step, I might have ended up next to you, four legs waving in the air. Not something I wish to add to my resumé, thank you. And I never would have had my breakfast on time."

I thought again about lunch. "What's so wrong about expectations?" I asked defensively. Surely the world would be a sad place without dreams and visions. I thought of how much I wanted to get my book published.

"A-HA!" my cow bellowed, all but knocking me back out into the snow. "Precisely my point."

"Excuse me?" I replied. Impatience was now chasing hunger, as my dream of a grilled cheese sandwich was melting into my stash of unrealized dreams, tangled up with my unpublished manuscript and—and—and...

"*There* is your wall, your fence, your entrapment," she said, shoving a soggy hoof in my direction. "If, on the other hand, you would simply enjoy looking at the soft, clean snow and *then* proceed to lunch; should you enjoy the process of writing, *and then—if it happens*—the process of publication, you would find that not only have you gone through the wall of regret and expectation, but you have also dissolved it along the way, allowing clarity of vision to enter in, and, might I venture, peace. And that, dear friend, is a plan to be proud of." She sighed deeply, extended her neck just so, and closed her eyes.

There really was nothing left to say. There was nothing to really think about either. Besides, my brain was tired. My thoughts had, miraculously, run dry. There was, however, snow in the air, now piling up like so many sparkling feathers, each snow flake a masterpiece in its own right—awesome!—the whole event deserving of my absolute attention and respect, moment by glistening moment. I found this oddly comforting, even satisfying. I rather liked Christina's plan.

But right now, my plan was calling for lunch.

18   LOSING FOOTING
ON THE PATH

"WOULD IT BE INAPPROPRIATE," CHRISTINA ASKED ME WHEN I STOMPED back out an hour later through the snow, sandwich in hand, "to inquire as to what all the ruckus was about just now?" I slowed my angry pacing to ponder her tranquil expression. In that one short hour an event occurred in my house that completely destroyed any sense of inner peace that I gained earlier.

"Why can't human beings be more like cows?" I remarked.

"I don't know," she responded. "In what manner would you prefer to emulate our species?"

I just stared at her in awe: One really had to admire her excellent grammar, wordy though she could be at times. How comforting to be in the presence of someone who understood the craft of good conversation, although I had to admit that I could be mighty sloppy about my own use of—

"And you think *I'm* wordy?" Christina asked, floating perfect enunciation around wads of leftover hay in her mouth.

"So, how we stand at this particular moment, my dear person," she said, "is that I am up by two questions and you are registering zero answers." She narrowed her eyes—one of her expressions for "cud-in-process / lesson commencing."

I turned again to stare at her. "Huh?"

Christina sighed deeply. I could be such a frustration to her at times. "I had previously asked you, *Would it be inappropriate to inquire as to...*"

"Yeah, okay; got that one. Yes, you can ask."

"You're very testy today," she said softly. "Anything you want to talk about?"

So now she was my therapist? Then I had to laugh, because the truth was, in her cowish ways, she was probably the finest therapist a confused individual could ever have. There was a polite cough from the barn.

"You did mention something about wishing humans were more like cows. That would be, in fact, my second question, if you recall." She settled in to wait for my response. And to wait... and wait... and wait. I was, you see, once again distracted by my own rampaging thoughts. After five minutes, another polite cough rolled forth from the hulking form before me.

"Oh, yes, yes—where were we? Therapists? You cows being so docile and accepting, I believe. Did I mention anything about cows being polite?" I was making a fool of myself, but felt unable to check my rambling. As usual, Christina rescued me in the kindest of manners.

"Humans have chosen a more complicated track of evolution," she began. "High-tech this and that, producing and accumulating whatever, dealing with—stuff—and certainly concurrently, highly self-involved and judgmental of others. And please forgive me mentioning humans forever being busy, busy, busy. Did I forget anything?"

"I doubt it," I said a bit coldly, taking a large, belligerent bite out of my sandwich.

She stopped in mid-swallow and turned to look squarely at me. "Not that I'm trying to hurt your feelings," she said quietly, "but frankly, cows just don't do any of the above. And, what I have mentioned is only the tip of the hay bale, and—what do you have there for lunch?"

"Grilled cheese and tomato on rye—and don't you mean *iceberg*?"

"No. I have nothing to which I can relate such an object."

"I see," I replied, trying to sound wise. But I didn't feel the part.

"Case in point," she continued. "How much simpler to draw upon a comparison with which I, being bovine, comprehend, whereas a large chunk of ice neither appeals to me, nor holds a whit of meaning."

"So if that's the case, dear heart," I said, wondering if I might actually be one up on her here, "if an iceberg is unfamiliar to you, how do you know it is a large chunk of ice?" There! See if she could maneuver out of that one.

"In your desperate need to be right," she replied, with all the grace of one who actually is and knows it, "you failed to hear what I said. *And I said*—a phenomenon such as an iceberg neither appeals to me, nor does it hold meaning for me. In a word, I have no use for one in my present life experience, being a cow at a sanctuary in the warm climes of the Mid-Atlantic, United States of America. *Now, a hay bale...*"

I opened my mouth to defend myself when she switched her tail across her back with that I'm-not-finished-yet expression. I worked on my sandwich instead.

"Of *course* I am familiar with the concept of icebergs. Being Cow, I know everything. Another way we differ from humans. But the truth is, humans know everything as well, only you all have forgotten most of it." Two burps and left ear back just so; I knew it was finally my turn to speak.

"So, shall I answer your first question?" I asked casually, trying to change the subject.

"I only wished to help, not to be nosy," she said, concentrating on a fly, awake way too early on such a cold day, that had landed rather shakily on her leg. "However, it did seem as if you were distressed after some sort of commotion that occurred before you came outside, and if I could be of any comfort—oh, excuse me one moment, I have another call..."

Well, I looked around for a telephone, but not even a cordless one seemed to be anywhere in our vicinity. I do realize cell phones are so small these days as to be easily missed; however... Not that I expected she *needed* a phone, being able to read minds and all, yet she did seem to be experiencing Call Waiting. On closer examination, however, I realized she was in solid mental conversation with said shivering fly.

There seemed to be a substantial amount of leg waving and foot wringing on the fly's part. And I thought I saw him produce a small handkerchief and dab at his eyes as if to emphasize whatever point was being discussed. In her usual serene manner, Christina gurgled, burped, rumbled, and sighed until quite obviously the tiny creature was greatly comforted and ready to move on with his life. They hugged (it's quite acceptable nowadays); that is, the fly wrapped his front feet around a few of the hairs on Christina's leg, and Christina simply thought *hug*, and her new client tottered off on icy feet back into the depths of the warm barn, much relieved. It was, in all, an awesome and rewarding experience for everyone.

"I beg your pardon," she said, turning to offer me her full attention once again. "So many in distress these days. You were saying?"

"Well," I began slowly, "I think you have just clarified a most important point for me." I was, once again, honestly impressed by my enormous companion with the endlessly compassionate heart.

"You see," I continued, "certain people I know make a habit of being not only disrespectful, but also verbally abusive to the animals in my care. The ruckus you asked about was over a comment just made by one who shall remain anonymous. Said person had the nerve to turn on little, ancient, frail Agatha and snarl at her—I *mean*, SNARL: 'Shut up, little dog!' Can you believe it? All she was doing was trying to say hello to said person. But all said person chose to hear was her barking." I felt my anger and grief once again overflowing the banks of my tolerance. Patience and forgiveness are not my strong suits when it comes to the animals.

"I understand," Christina said quietly. "And how did Agatha react to such an attack?"

I wiped my eyes. "Oh, you know how dogs are; they keep on wagging their tails. It takes some consistent abuse to change their loving attitude. And that makes it so much harder for me to tolerate such terrible behavior. No one deserves to be spoken to that way. It's wrong, just really wrong."

Christina went silent. She would be in agreement, I knew. I waited for her profound and supportive response. "Not necessarily," she replied, almost inaudibly, but she was quite sure of her words.

I, however, was stunned.

"You made mention of a difference between cows and humans, am I correct?"

"Yes."

"Then you must know that though we appear slow and stupid, it is only because we are taking the time and opportunity to see everything as it relates to the whole of life, the whole of isness, if you will. To see in such a manner requires a quiet, watchful attitude, one that is completely without judgment. And what we have learned as a species is that in truth, there are no such concepts as *right* or *wrong*."

I was lost, confused, emotionally exhausted. Sensing this, she leaned against me, letting her soft cheek rest easily against my shoulder—her ultimate sign of affection. "This is difficult for humans to understand, and you don't need to feel guilty or ashamed about your own views relative to mine," Christina said. "But please hear what you have just said to me: *Agatha simply continued to wag her tail.* She, too, is without judgment, accepting all beings, even humans, with unlimited love."

"But what about animals who are so beaten or neglected that they become frightened or vicious?" I asked.

"Cows, too, are often abused, not fed properly, hit or shocked repeatedly, considered as nothing more than commodities on a fluctuating market. And I haven't even mentioned the holding pens or slaughterhouses. Price-per-pound is a tough way to be thought of. However, we do also know that the present suit we wear, called 'cow's body,' is not who we really are. And who we really are is always safe, always loved in a manner that far transcends earthly affection/love. When an animal or human is pushed to a point beyond bearing, a critical decision will have to be made: to succumb, or to defend oneself; either way is bound to lead to the separation of body and soul. A welcome relief in such a case."

"Do you mean *death?*" I whispered.

"Yes."

"Oh," I said, through now-uncontrollable tears. "How terrible!"

"Not at all," Christina replied once again in that even, knowledgeable tone. "When one's work is done, one gets to leave. It's okay." She dried my left cheek with her ear. "You said a moment ago that I had clarified a most important point for you. And how was that?"

"Without hesitation or discrimination, you paid full, respectful, and immediate attention to that fly, as if he were the most important creature in the entire universe," I replied. "Nothing of what or who he is or what is generally thought of flies kept you from helping him. That is the way I want to be, all the time."

Christina chuckled. "You mean, I didn't snarl, 'Shut up, little insect!' " And that made me grin.

"Better than being so furious, isn't it?" she remarked. "If you can learn to step aside, not necessarily from others, but from the hurtful things they say or do, and try to see them as souls just like yourself, struggling to find their spiritual footing on an often-rocky path, you will find that you smile more and rage less. Does that make sense to you?" I took the last bite of my sandwich and reached for the bag of chocolate chip cookies in my pocket. "I guess so," I said thoughtfully. "But why does it have to be so hard to remember?"

19 WHAT ANGER FEELS LIKE

EARLY THE NEXT MORNING, YET ANOTHER FRIGID JANUARY DAY, I asked Christina yet another question. "Please tell me more about anger." Obviously (for me, at least), this was an open-ended topic of soul development that needed further work. But she only observed me with those deep, somber eyes; silence domed the barn, often her way of asking for clarification. I approached from another angle: "Do you *ever* get angry?"

"No."

"Why not?" I replied skeptically. How could any creature—human or otherwise—who so clearly felt love and affection as well as pain and despair as she did, not feel—

"Not in my experience," she interrupted in her clipped manner. "It is my understanding that only members of your species demonstrate anger."

"Hold on a minute!" I cried, and at my request, she stopped chewing her cud. I had forgotten how literal this cow could be. She studied me with intently. "Tough morning again?"

"You know it," I replied bitterly. Indeed, I had arrived at her stall from yet another less-than-amusing encounter with the same person. Anger had been my first reactive response—to the situation and the individual—followed by anger at myself for getting angry. I was exhausted, and it was only eight o'clock. But the *other* truth was that Christina did, in fact, already know all of this, being able to read my thoughts just as other animals around me do. At this notion, I thought I saw a tiny smile cross her eyes. "Are you pitying me?" I asked defensively. Obviously I wasn't yet ready to let go of my morning's tirade.

"Don't know how to do that one either," she said thoughtfully. "Just trying to relate."

"Okay, then, what if I were to kick you; wouldn't you get angry then?" More silence. Then—

"No." That was all: a soft, barely audible but definite word/thought sent trembling between us. It landed, painfully, in my heart. Christina sighed deeply, raising herself to her knees, then almost as if levitating, she was suddenly on her feet.

"But if you would call me Friend," she said as she walked out of the barn away from me, "don't abuse me."

Horrified, I remained in the hay, simply staring after her. In her literal way, had she thought I could ever actually be capable of hurting her?

"Of course not," she said over her shoulder. "It's just time for my snack."

Sacred time was upon us, when food gatherers and grazers hit the grasslands. With her face pinned to the ground, I knew our discussion was over, and out of respect, I took my unhappy self and left. I had much to mull over. For the rest of the day I chewed on my anger, alternately berating myself for fostering such feelings, letting them go, taking them back, and amplifying them. By afternoon feeding time, I found myself limping, both body and soul, to the barn.

"Is it pleasant?" Christina asked me, as I piled hay into the corner of her stall.

"What?" I replied, quite disgruntled. Now it was my turn to be clipped and somber. Of course, there was nothing more to the conversation with Christina now full throttle into her dinner. It wasn't until I had finished filling water buckets, cleaning stalls, and tending to the donkeys that she gave forth the next word.

"Anger."

"Anger, *what?*" I said as I pulled loose hay up around the bale. I had forgotten her original question and had allowed my mind to rumble around some more through the morning's explosive events.

"Is anger pleasant? You spend so much time with anger, it

must be something you like. Just the way you say you like to be with me so much."

Because she seemed to be genuinely interested (in truth, cows are genuine about everything), and because she was willing to converse at such an unaccustomed hour, I set the pitchfork aside and leaned on the hay bale, my nose an inch from hers.

"No." I said calmly. "I *adore* you, but I very much dislike being angry. Two different things entirely."

Her jaws moved counterclockwise three times, followed by a belch and a loud glug as her cud found its proper stomach chamber. "Humans are complicated," she stated, just as the molars swung into action again.

I couldn't help but chuckle. "That's because we're the superior species," I reminded her.

"Okay." She turned and walked back to her water bucket, drinking it half away. Darn if she hadn't taken me literally again! What was a person to do with her cow, anyway?

"Didn't you know I was joking?" I called after her. She swung her head up and around to stare silently at me again.

"I know," I said, shaking my head. "You don't relate to humor either, do you?"

Christina lowered her head to the ground outside her stall, never losing eye contact. "Did I ever tell you the joke about the farmer and his cow?" she said, a mischievous look brimming over from her dark eyes. "There was this farmer, you see, and he had a cow he was planning to take to the market, but the cow—"

"Hold it!" I shouted, holding up my hand. "I thought you didn't relate to humor."

"*You* said that, not me. So, this cow—"

"You mean to say cows tell jokes?"

"Oh," she said, raising her head high in disappointment. "You've heard this one."

I banged my head on the hay bale. I just couldn't stop laughing; the look on her face was enough to turn a slab of granite into pudding. "No, no!" I cried, tears running down my face. "Please, go on!"

There was a notable pause in the dialogue as Christina gathered her ample frame to her full height of forty-seven inches. "I don't understand what you find so amusing," she said in a somewhat terse tone. "I hadn't gotten to the punch line yet."

"I know, I know!" I could barely squeak out my words between my by-now raucous hooting. "It's just that I didn't know cows told jokes, and you look so funny doing it!" I was busy slumping to the ground in hysterics when I felt the Earth shift direction beneath me. Christina was—yes, indeed, *stomping* away, nose held high with something like steam issuing from her ears. Could it be that she was the first cow, ever, to experience—*anger?*

"I didn't mean to hurt your feelings," I called after her, but she was in a huff, and, it being a new experience for her, she seemed to be enjoying it.

"Shhhhh..." she said ever so softly. "I'm relating."

Next day, 9:42 A.M.: Ms. Cow and her human are back in the barn. Flies in place, sun ever so welcome on this chilly day, cud maneuvers in full swing. "You know, Christina," I said to my sweet and massive friend, "I'm not angry anymore. How about you?"

"Never was," she replied, pointedly looking the other way.

"Then why the theatrics yesterday?"

"Just wanted to see what anger felt like."

"Okay," I said graciously, "have it your way."

We contemplated Herds Mountain for a longish time, brooding on important subjects pertinent to cows and humans. At last I shifted to a more-comfortable position and spoke aloud. "I have a great joke to tell you," I began. "Once there was an oak tree who wanted to marry a spruce."

Christina extended one leg in anticipation, that mischievous look filling up her face. "But before he could," she broke in, "he *pined* away!"

"Oh, you've heard that one," I said, quite disappointed.

"Yeah," she replied, switching her tail back and forth in merriment, "but have you heard the one about the bishop and the pig?"

20 IT'S LOVE

I DO, TRUTHFULLY, ADORE CHRISTINA—ALWAYS HAVE, ALWAYS WILL, for the rest of my existence, in or out of this physical body. The great thing about cows, as well as many other animals, is that they know when someone loves them and yet they never take advantage of it. No manipulation such as *I'll love you back if...* or *I will love you when...* or even more insidious (in my opinion, anyway), If you really loved me, you would... Fill in the blanks; humans do it all the time.

Not cows. They either love you or they could care less about you. If they are abused or loved, they will remember. Cows stand in one spot and watch, sometimes for a long time. They aren't being stupid or brainless; they're simply observing. They're reading the signs and signals around them and processing the information. They can feel great fear and panic; they can experience despair and grief, especially over lost calves or mothers, depending on which one is gone and which one remains.

And decidedly, cows understand about love. Christina, who reads me like an Internet website, knows the struggles I have with love—accepting other people's love for me, being able to offer love to those (people) who would consciously try to emotionally hurt or neglect me. She knows I work hard all the time to be the Love I know we always are, on a practical, manifested level. All of my struggles with love disappear when I am with an animal. Love flows so easily between us, a mutual field of respect and appreciation. We are each other's fan club, at least among the animals in my family. The wild ones are usually timid or apprehensive. It's difficult to trust one human's love when the human species in general has so little respect for them. But not all people, of course. In the future maybe the wild ones will learn to trust us again. Christina once told me that cows as a group understand that people will one day shed the erroneous belief that human beings are superior to everyone and everything else on the planet. Cows are patient folk; they are waiting for us to grow up. But wild animals just want us to leave. Anger, Christina then told me, is not the opposite of love. There is no opposite to love. Love really is all there is; it's just that one's perception, and subsequent willingness to act on that perception (also called intent), will color how one sees or does not see love. Cows know this; people work at it. Being angry simply means we are confused about love. One day the confusion will be cleared up and there will be only the perception of love as it truly is.

There is hope for the human race, according to Christina. And that means there is hope for the planet to survive intact. But we struggling humans had better start communicating more with one another about love rather than hate and crime and disease, and all those other so-called "negative" things.

Turn off the news, Christina advises. And open your ears, your eyes, your hearts and voice to what really matters.

It's love.

21   RADIO-ACTIVE COW

AND SOON ENOUGH, VALENTINE'S DAY—MY FAVORITE HOLIDAY— ARRIVED IN Batesville. As I approached my beloved bovine on this fine day, Christina rose to her feet, greeting me with a swish of her tail. Then quite abruptly she turned and headed straight to the middle of her pasture where she raised her nose to the sky and announced: "This is WCOW 2746 on your FM dial, coming to you from the The Animals' Peace Garden in Batesville, Virginia, and you are listening to Ask the Cow. I am Christina, your host; are there any callers, puh-leeze?"

If I rolled my eyes it was only because my beloved bovine looked absolutely ridiculous with her head straight up and back, her eyes shining as if she had indulged in too much caffeine. "What are you doing?" I asked, stepping swiftly to the left as she flew past me in one of her spurts of merriment, tail straight out except for that fly-swatter part at the end that flops back and forth in the wind.

Christina skidded to a halt directly in front of me. "It's time for me to do my talk show," she replied, in a manner that seemed to indicate I should be well aware of this fact.

"And what do cows know about talk shows, let alone radio?"

"You might just be surprised," she said, taking a moment to study her left front hoof. "Radio happens to be one of my favorite hobbies—after watercolor painting, of course."

"All right," I countered, cutting her off. "I realize cows know everything. However, personally, now I think you're just being silly."

"Why?" The eyes downshifted to look straight through me.

"Because..."

But I could tell Christina suddenly had something very important to say. This was always the case when her gaze narrowed and she began shuffling her feet. At such times I intuitively sensed that I was in the presence of a wise and ancient master, certainly an animal of sizable proportion who could, if she so chose, plow me over in an instant. I decided to be respectful for a change.

"What is the purpose of radio?" she asked quietly.

"Entertainment and information," I replied.

"Precisely. And what is another word for what radio does?"

"Communicate?"

"Correct again," she said. "And that is all I am doing. Communicating. Only, I don't need the equipment to do so." She lifted that left front hoof in an awkward manner and waved it at me—not easily done when one has chubby, short extremities. "A fine art, a talent to be appreciated. Care to call in a question? We are on the air!"

Well, what could I say? Sure didn't see any studio; and no headphones enveloped her ears. And where there *could* have been an eighty-foot tower, I saw only the gatepost. I was a bit skeptical. To such a thought (which she reads like a page), she said nothing, but was it coincidence that she suddenly felt the necessity to make a deposit to her manure account?

Hey, I could play along. What else to do with the day? "Okay," I said as seriously as I could. "I am placing a call to Ask the Cow. My questions are: How do cattle communicate? What do they communicate about? And how relevant is said communication to the overall destiny of planet Earth?" If that didn't stump her, nothing would.

But Christina lowered her head and launched right in: "I will answer in the precise order in which the questions have been asked. Please understand, Caller, that you have indeed introduced some interesting and vital thoughts here, and while we will try to answer as fully and completely as possible, this may take several shows to complete. I am assuming you will be available to tune in tomorrow as well?"

Darn, she sure did seem serious about this radio thing. Or, was she just stringing me along? "Sure, sure," I replied, waving my left front foot (um, hand) back at her. Perhaps that was a signal of some sort.

"Communication is the key to fully understanding and accurately supporting the planetary infrastructure, and is of the utmost importance if we, as a global community, are to manifest peace, cooperation, and, most important, love between all beings who reside therein (humans invited only if they straighten up and start behaving themselves). Do you follow me?"

"Sure, sure," I reiterated, realizing instantly that I was one of those she was referring to. Removing the sarcasm from my voice, I rephrased my answer. "Yes," I said, feeling impressively intelligent.

"*Humility*," Christina continued sternly, "is an essential element of positive and constructive communication, and while effortless for cows, seems to be a stumbling block for humans. So how do we cows communicate? As you do, Caller, through body language, audible sound, and vibration. We, however, possess an ability few of you have. We are able to send and *receive* mental images, thoughts, colors, and sounds well beyond your range of perception."

"Aha!" I cried, jumping up and down excitedly. "So, what happened to humility?" Christina barely moved an eyelash.

"Did I say that made us *better* than you?"

"Er—no."

"Exactly. You do things that we can't—or choose not to—do."

I couldn't resist: "Such as host real radio talk shows?"

"I was thinking of shopping."

"Oh."

"But your point brings up another angle to the difference between how we communicate—and what—and why," said Christina. "Remember— these are your questions, Caller... . What?" Christina asked, somewhat annoyed. I was frantically waving my hand in the air as if in school. She never did like to have a thought interrupted.

"Why do you keep referring to me as 'Caller'? I have a name, and you know what it is."

Christina shuffled some more, sighed deeply, burped. Obviously, I was touching a nerve.

"In radio," she began patiently, "callers to talk shows are referred to simply as 'Caller' to protect their identity. Presumably, you should know this? However, if you wish to be addressed by a specific name, you may choose one which will accomplish the same end. And that would be?"

"Bob."

Perhaps I was making a fuss over nothing. "Yes, you are," the now-impatient hulk in front of me replied.

Sometimes I did wish she would not read my mind.

"All right, *Bob*," she continued, putting, I thought, a bit of sarcasm into my new name, "I was about to say, humans have noisy, busy minds, thoughts about this, that, and the other all confused with past, present, and future—nothing much relevant to the moment. And oh my, all that negative stuff! All this confusion and chatter and bickering and fighting and backstabbing is sent out on the airwaves just the same as your spoken words. Gets a bit deafening, if you know what I mean."

"So?" I shot back. Now I was getting defensive.

"Only that the difference between humans and cows regarding communication is that we have quiet minds—peaceful, focused, present-oriented minds—and so our thoughts and words are few, select, carefully chosen, constructive, and thus supportive of yes, the overall enhancement of the global community. Less said the better, I believe someone of your kind once wrote?"

I didn't have anything to say in rebuttal. She was correct, of course. Most of the animals I have encountered, both wild and domestic, are beings of few words, my cow-companion included. And thus very wise. I bowed my head. "To communicate, whether to one, or many," Christina said softly, "is a gift one can give forth. Those of the non-human world instinctively know, and choose to communicate in a loving, supportive manner. You know, the 'we are one' type of thing. While it sounds dreadfully New Age, there is a great deal of merit to it. How one chooses to communicate affects everything and everyone, everywhere; no equipment, including radio towers, necessary."

"That's a powerful responsibility," I said, with genuine awe.

"Yes," she replied, lowering her poundage to the ground. "And cow talk shows take that responsibility very seriously." Her eyes closed; I assumed our discussion was complete. I started to tiptoe away when her wonderfully broad, pink nose rose again as if to study something in the air. "Next caller, puh-leeze," she stated with authority. After a brief and intense moment, she continued: "Yes, go ahead; you're on the air."

As I turned to go back inside where chores awaited me, I heard her cough politely, then say to whatever frequency she was now tuned into:

"Your question is, 'Why do humans shop?'" She shifted her mass for maximum comfort. "Please understand, Caller, that you have introduced an interesting and vital thought here, and while we will try to answer as fully and completely as possible..."

22   BUILD ME A SNOWCOW

YOU KNOW THE BEST KIND OF LATE-MARCH SNOW: MEDIUM-SIZED flakes falling fast and thick, just damp enough to stick together and build a snow fort, stock it with snowballs, and after a sure and swift victory, fashion the perfect snowman. One Wednesday had it all: temps holding at 32 degrees Fahrenheit, snowing so smoothly the mountains disappeared; everything a silent, silky blur of tumbling iridescence. And I was hard at work.

I rolled the first hunk of snow until it was so big I had to put my hip against it to make the last turn. Then I set it just right—where my snowman would face the road and greet each passerby with good cheer. His finished self would be visionary, I had decided. No wooly hat and scarf for my creation; he was born to be a poet, reading verse to the trees and birds. A mixed-fiber burgundy cardigan would wrap about his ample body and a French beret sit slanted atop his snow-white head. Being a nonsmoker (health-conscious, of course), instead of a pipe, he would hold a book close to his chest, and with the other arm outstretched, he would appear to recite words of true love to the world. I would name him Percy.

I turned back to start rolling the chunk of snow that would be Percy's upper body. One second my immediate world was mysterious—shrouded in swirling whiteness. The next second: a hulking mass was pushing toward me, completely snow-covered except for a dash of auburn down the shuffling legs. The apparition emerged from the mysterious beyond and halted abruptly in front of me. Large, despondent brown eyes peered at me from snow-encrusted eyelashes. "It was *spring* yesterday," a sad voice murmured. Then the bulky form belched in a familiar and endearing way.

"Yes. Yes it was," I replied, undaunted. True, it had been a lovely day on Tuesday, reaching into the sixties. I had remarked to No One Listening that the grass was even turning quite green for March. But a touch of late winter keeps one alert and guessing, I assumed. If nothing else—

"I suppose it's good for the spring hay crop and gardens," the now shivering beast said with a sigh, completing my thought. No question now who I was conversing with.

"See?" I said pleasantly, trying to cheer up my disgruntled cow, "I'm building a snowman. Want to help?" The look returned from the being before me was less supportive than I would have expected from such a normally placid and balanced creature. Perhaps it was her day off.

"His name is Percy," I continued cheerily. "He's a poet, inspired by nature."

"I suppose he gives freely of his work?" Christina asked. She seemed to be perking up.

"Absolutely," I replied. Things were shifting here. Was my beloved cow turning the simple act of snowman-building into another one of her life lessons?

"Uh-huh," she said, once again reading my thoughts while nodding and gulping. Cud followed. I always thought she should write a handbook—*Things to Be Chewed on With Care.*

"And, being earthbound," she continued, with more animation now, "he understands about strengths and weaknesses? Does he feel passionately about the sanctity of all life? Does he—"

"Yeah, okay, sure," I said hastily. Percy was to be, after all, a snowman. He wasn't running for poet laureate. Christina was obviously on a roll—but not the kind I needed right then, the kind that binds snowflake to snowflake until you have a firm yet well-toned midsection for said snowman. Never mind; Christina was not even reading my thoughts by this point. She circled widely and carefully around Percy's beginnings, as if pondering an as-yet-uncarved block of stone.

"Hmmm," she said softly. More circling, more hmmm-ing, while the day was moving rapidly toward dusk. I decided to return to my happy task and began rolling the next chunk of Percy's anatomy.

"Wait!" the trembling bovine behind me cried. Was she cold? Ill? My heart raced with concern.

"Does Percy understand about vulnerability and impermanence?" she demanded. "Is your intended poet well versed in the concept of immortality?"

Oh, not cold or ill. Only her inner philosopher tuning up. I breathed easily again.

"Please!" Christina declared, stomping her left front foot, not the best sign. "I mean it. Look!" she said, nodding her head toward Percy's abbreviated form. "You have begun to create not just a snowman, but a *Snow Someone*! Someone with energy, name, and passion. A poet, and by your description, not one who writes for profit and fame, but for the love of the word as art and communication, for *love*, for goodness' sake. How can Percy be just any other snowman?"

I looked first at Percy's bare beginnings, and then at my by-now-exuberant teacher. And with utmost respect I asked her, "So, what's your point?"

She stared at me with that bland expression cows are so famous for, the one that tends to get them labeled as "dumb animals." And then up came the cud again. Slow rotation of the jaws. Silence. Lowering of the eyelashes.

I knew I was in trouble.

"Forget building Percy. That's my strong advice," she said quietly.

"But..." She lifted that left front foot and placed it just so, an inch from the new ball of snow. "If you are going to create someone, anyone, create with conscience and build me a snowcow." And she turned and started to walk back to the barn. I looked from Percy's meager start in life to Christina as she began to once again melt into the veil of falling snow. And I thought, and thought, and thought.

"Think about the sun!" came drifting through the flakes.

All right. The sun. My turn to "hmmm." Yes, tomorrow the forecast called for the sun to reemerge; spring, in its more temperate persona, would return. The snow would melt and... Oh! Percy! My poet! He would dissolve back to earth, still pitifully proclaiming the importance of love. I turned to yell in the direction of the barn, but a cough and hiccup behind me caught my words half born and I sat down abruptly in the snow.

The soft voice and garlic breath of my familiar friend embraced me from just above: "Percy, gentle soul that he is destined, by your vision, to become, would not understand why one day, *this* day, he is Poet Extraordinaire, and the next, a mere puddle on a swampy lawn. He is to be fashioned, after all, in the likeness of humanity, is he not?"

I nodded, dismally. I had held such great plans for my Percy.

"Nonsense," Christina replied, eavesdropping on my brain. "The poet shall live, but let him enjoy existence as a cow poet, a creature who is experienced at *living* as Love, not just the purveyor of words. Cows know that whatever is their current lot, whether it be material existence or meltdown, a true poet lives, no matter what. Cows are so much better at handling the ebb and flow of life, the emergence of energy into form, the dissolving of form back into fluid energy. We have that stuff down pat. Believe me, Percy would thank you."

With that parting statement, my companion once again trod northward to the warmth of her stall and hay, leaving me to ponder on how to construct a cow from snow.

"Well..." I heard her voice, drifting through the air. "If I were you, I would start with the body, *then* add the legs and head—don't forget the tail—and that cardigan would be a nice touch."

You know the best kind of snow, when that last fling of late winter keeps one alert and guessing, if nothing else...

23   ENTERING THE HEART

SURE ENOUGH, MY MAGNIFICENT SNOWCOW MELTED THE NEXT DAY in the predictable rebound of spring. As I watched the cardigan, once so protectively draped across the snowy shoulders, sink further and further to the ground, I felt an immense, familiar sadness rising concurrently within me. By afternoon, all that was left was the sweater. I was bereft; not for the loss of the snowcow, but for what she—and her evaporation—had suddenly symbolized for me: all those creatures who had so blessed my life over the years, only to seemingly evaporate into the unknown, leaving behind the favorite blanket, bowl, collar, and toy. I began walking in circles around the sweater, desperate in my grief.

"Is there a problem?" Ensconced by the barn, Christina asked me this question in her usual docile manner. I stopped my incessant pacing long enough to notice that her eyes seemed somewhat crossed. Still, her head followed all my steps, around and around on the lawn—around and around and...

I stopped mid-pace directly in front of her.

"Clear as a cloud," she remarked, returning to her traditional clipped and irritating way of giving out only half of what was percolating in her brain.

"As in?" I asked warily.

"If you will simply employ leaf green," she replied brightly, "everything will be fine."

"I haven't a clue what you're talking about," I said rather coolly. Give that cow any rope and she will lead you away into confusion.

"Sit a moment," Christina said, gesturing with her head to the ground beside her. I felt so very sleepy. Despite my efforts to stay awake, I sat back against one of the wooden fence posts. The day was cool but the sun was warm, and the wind had died back—tolerable indeed for a spring day. Suddenly, I was exhausted, and tears started to flow. Christina turned her head to the side, studying me intently. There was no sign of pity, or really, of any emotion from her, but deep warmth and love flowed in waves around me.

"Tell me," she whispered softly, "what hurts you so much."

How did she know these things? I wondered.

"By your colors," she said, lowering her head to look down on me as if she were peering over bifocals. Despite my all-consuming gloom, this image made me smile.

"Do we need to review about the Garden?" she asked kindly.

"No, not really," I replied, feeling at the moment that lessons and words were not going to take away my grief. Then the words just tumbled out of me: "I miss my friends." I hardly expected her to understand, since for her, life is just an ongoing process, in this world or beyond. I told her so, to which she replied: "Cows know everything."

"Then perhaps you can tell me how to get out of this sadness, and explain why it keeps coming up for me, just when I think I understand what life and death are about?"

"I can help," Christina said. "I will not give you the answers, but I can offer the tools to help you find those answers for yourself."

No. I wanted the shortcut, with little or no effort. I was plain worn out. The look in her eyes told me I was out of luck. Did my cow have no mercy here?

"On the contrary," she shot back. "True mercy supports and educates—e-ducare: to lead outward from—"

"So now you know Latin, too?" I asked

"—within you," she continued undisturbed by my sarcasm. "In fact, within all beings stands the ultimate source of information that will help you solve every problem, every situation, down to the most minute inconvenience, and answer every query you have, even to the most mundane. Do you wish to experience that source?"

Why not? The day was young; I had nowhere to go and no money to spend. Perhaps a diversion would be comforting.

"Sure," I replied. I had intended to add something smart, but suddenly I felt so very sleepy. Despite my efforts to stay awake, I sat back against one of the wooden fence posts and fell asleep, immediately entering a strange, but pleasant dream. And in my dream I was moving very quickly, although I couldn't tell where I was going, only that I was traveling in no familiar direction, and oddly enough, without sensation of speed or motion, a most peculiar dichotomy. And—I appeared to be moving alone; there was no sign of my bovine companion anywhere.

Still, I felt no fear. Intuitively I knew I could trust whatever was happening if Christina was behind it. No dumb animal, she is a cow of knowledge and skill who is also humble and discreet enough to not flaunt her exceptional nature: sure of herself, but not showy about it. That's my cow.

And so I trusted this dream. Everything was now melding into a seemingly spherical field of energy, a flowing together—an intermeshing of all form, thought, word, and action. Nothing had definitive line or density, but a translucent quality that evoked joy in every part of me. I realized that I, too, was part of the energy flow as my body parts kept rearranging themselves in different colors, patterns of light and dark, shape and shadow. As I observed this peculiar situation I again felt no concern, only satisfaction that all seemed to be in perfect order, as if according to some master plan. Was it Christina's? Or, my own, subconsciously formulated on a level I was not even aware of? The possibilities were endless and intriguing, and in the particular state I found myself in, quite a wonderful adventure.

"Enjoying yourself?" a deep, resonant voice said beside me, ringing sweetly through my head as I turned from violet to deep purple and back to burgundy. Christina floated into view.

"Oh, there you are!" I exclaimed. Her form appeared to be undulating as well, and at certain points of contact, our energy bodies flowed together, causing a tickling sensation, and I spontaneously giggled. As I did so, bubbles of iridescent colors floated out from my mouth and moved through us both.

"Now I will have you practice a specific exercise," Christina announced with authority.

Still giggling, I replied: "Yes, ma'am!"

"Close your eyes," she continued, my silliness making her sigh. *How could she be serious with all those wonderful bubbles bouncing through us?* "And visualize the color leaf green."

Okay, done—easy enough to do in a dream! And as I did, an extraordinary thing occurred: warmth and light of unmatched brilliance poured from the area of my heart. This was a sensation beyond anything I had ever experienced, in either a dream or when awake; I wanted it to last forever.

"Now," Christina seemed to be saying, "with this exercise, you have activated your heart chakra, or energy center—the aspect of your total beingness that is relative to both your physical heart and your spiritual heart. The green represents Life of an eternal nature, that which you experience no matter which body, or which dimension you are currently experiencing—or, for that matter, experiencing simultaneously. But that discussion is for another time. Right now, focus on the green color and your heart energy."

Goodness, she was suddenly quite wordy. I wanted her to be quiet so that I could enjoy the sensations of the color, but she continued nonetheless. I guessed it must be important that she do so, or she would have honored my thoughts.

"When you are in trouble, or just seeking clarity on any matter or concern," she said, "go to that color, and then go to your heart in your mind as if calling forth an old friend. Recall the sensation you are now experiencing and ask your questions. Your heart is the center of all knowledge and all wisdom, without all the nonsensical chatter and confusion of the brain." She paused, turning into a palette of the most extraordinary pastel colors. "Each and every being, in and out of form on Earth and everywhere, contains Heart—not the physical aspect of the heart as you understand it, but the spirit-ethereal aspect. That's why there is nothing anywhere that does not contain that same center and source of wisdom and knowledge. If you want the short term for all of this, it's Pure Love, capital 'P', capital 'L.' "

"Do fleas and ticks have Heart? And what about ear mites?" I asked, recalling some difficulty my dogs and cats had experienced in past seasons with these little critters.

"There are no exceptions," came the stern reply.

I felt foolish then, asking such a stupid, careless question. And as I allowed that guilt into my awareness, instantly the colors vanished, the bubbles dissolved, the warmth subsided, and I found myself once again wide awake, back sitting on the chilly, damp ground next to Christina's very physical hulk. I was distraught; she was chewing cud.

"What happened?" I asked, staring directly into her wide and handsome face.

"You thought less of yourself," she said. "Simply put, at the place of the Heart, all beings are equally their true selves, being Love. When you think less of yourself, or any other—in other words, without love and/or respect—then your judgment shifts your awareness back to the illusion you and so many of your species experience most of the time. To return to the place of the Heart, all you need to do is know yourself and all others in the highest, most loving, and respectful manner. Dr. Schweitzer put it nicely: Reverence for Life."

"You've read his books?"

"Not had the privilege," she replied nonchalantly.

"Then how—"

"Knew him when he was at Lambarene—during my last life, of course. I was his favorite cat. We inspired each other, actually. Good man; you should look him up when you drop this life."

Her eyes were closing now, her chewing interspersed with comfortable burps and belches that were just that— ongoing digestion in the ultimate stream of life. Our session was ending. But despite my intriguing dream of traveling into the Heart, in my brain I still felt frantic and sad. I was, indeed, lost in thought.

Christina stirred, poking one chubby leg forward and shifting slightly to the left, her signal that it was time to nap deeply. Perhaps it was mercy that prodded her to speak again before turning in.

"Okay, one more time: Step one—think green; once there, step two—call on your heart as your friend, for it is. Step three—know yourself to be the Love you really are; not in an egotistical way, you understand, but as the being of spirit that is your true nature. You will know when you are there, as the signposts are clearly marked. And when you do, step four—ask your questions, expect answers, and all else in your life will fall neatly into place. Oh, and step five? Always write down your dreams."

24   PLENITUDE AND PEACE

I WAS WILLING TO TRY ALL THE STEPS CHRISTINA HAD JUST GIVEN ME. MAYBE if I went for a walk and thought about the Heart as my friend, I would come closer to finding peace. How elusive could this really be?

A log in our small woods, warmed by the sun, offered me a seat and I accepted. I pulled a pen and small notebook from my pocket and recorded my dream. Then I sat back and closed my eyes. I could have heard the Carolina wren calling above me in the pines, felt the warm air cross my forehead, or drawn in the cheering aroma of cedar boughs, but I missed it all. Despite my intentions, my mind had jumped from one area of sadness to another of worry, all within seconds. I was, once again, literally lost in thought.

"Need a compass?" a soft voice said from behind me.

"Excuse me?" I replied, not needing to turn around. The heady garlic breath pouring over me identified my visitor as my beloved cow, who then burped pleasantly as she strode around to look me in the eye.

"A compass, my dear," she repeated. "You seem to have lost your way in a tangle of concern, frustration, and confusion. My goodness, it's dusky in your brain right now! Perhaps a sturdy flashlight would help as well."

She seemed to be searching through—pockets?—on her left side, pockets (or a garment of any sort) invisible to *my* eyes, but nonetheless, obviously of substance to her. "Ah, here we go!" she said triumphantly, producing, well, yes, nothing, but shoving the "nothing" toward me with her left hoof. "And happily, *this* flashlight comes with a complete set of instructions written in English, French, Greek, and Bovinese."

"Well," I replied dryly, "can't read any of it without my glasses—even if I had the slightest idea of what you are talking about." I dropped my chin into my hands and felt very sorry for myself.

"Hmmm, yes, I see your point," Christina said smoothly. "Perhaps I could read the instructions to you." She appeared to be turning the pages of something propped up against the log. "It says here on page two to 'grasp the flashlight firmly in one hand and step boldly forward with assurance.' And there is an asterisk here; it says, 'Be sure the flashlight is turned on.' "

Instead of trying to grasp anything, I held up my hand to stop her. She didn't notice, or simply chose not to.

" 'Generously'—it does say that here," she continued, " 'offer a hand-up to anyone behind you. By doing so, be assured that this flashlight will always provide all the direction in life you will ever need.' "

"I can't grasp something I don't see, and I don't need a flashlight. It's daytime, for goodness' sake!" I had far too much on my mind to play games with a cow, who, it would seem, had far too much time on her hands/hooves.

Christina let forth an enormous and fragrant sigh. "My dear student," she began patiently, shifting her feet in a rather enchanting way (her version of line dancing?), "it is precisely the 'far too much on your mind' part that cries loudly for illumination. I am surprised you even noticed that it's daytime."

Well, she was right. She always is. And that one thought alone riled me substantially, because it appeared to me that in her opinion, I was "messing up."

"Tell me about wealth," she said, jumping into another subject without explanation. I shrugged my shoulders and stared at my feet.

"What do you want to know?" I asked.

"Do you consider yourself wealthy?"

"Financially, no; in many other ways, very much so. Good friends, for instance."

"And why not financially?" she asked, bouncing words back at me with lightning speed. Her eyes never left me.

"Don't know, but it worries me constantly."

"You feel you don't deserve wealth, am I correct?"

"Maybe."

"And so you mentally push it away. You want and need that income, but then you reject it, only because you reject yourself."

Back to me messing up.

"Hardly," Christina replied. "Only something for you to work on. The lightness and ease you seek financially or otherwise is being blocked by the confusion in your brain."

I opened my mouth to dispute her theory, but she seemed otherwise suddenly distracted.

"Hmmm," she said thoughtfully, dropping her eyes to her toes. "Just as I thought."

"What?" I asked, hoping she had a positive suggestion for me.

"There's a rock in my foot; that's why it's been hurting and making me limp." She leaned down and chewed on her right foot. "Got it!" she exclaimed happily, setting the small rock by my foot. When she looked back up at me, I was frowning hard.

Christina, however, has a way of "doing her eyes" to create the effect of smiling kindly. "Now, see if you can figure it all out," she said. She turned to face the sun and settled down in the deep layer of pine needles surrounding us. She appeared to be in no hurry to explain anything to me. I picked up the smallish granite rock (which I did clearly see) and turned it over in my hands. It had jagged edges and hurt my hand a bit if I closed my fist around it. But glints of mica in its multiple facets reflected the sun's light, and I continued to study it.

"It's really a pretty stone, isn't it?" Christina said without opening her eyes. "Of itself, *not* wedged in my foot, I would have to say it is perfect and stunning. A keeper."

"You collect rocks?" I asked incredulously.

"No, they belong to the soil," she replied. "I will give this one back to the Earth, but I *will* keep the memory of our meeting and her beauty. And for that, I consider myself very wealthy."

"Which has to do what with finances?"

"Oh, not a thing; and everything," she said evenly. "What do you see as the difference, or similarity, between this beautiful yet sharp-edged stone, and gaining a substantial financial income?" I continued to turn the small rock in my hand, feeling the points press into my skin, watching the light sparkling off the mica—pain, and pleasure; feelings of anxiety and nervous anticipation for the discomfort of my hand slowly overtaking any awe and joy for the ancient, brilliant being I held there. After a while I laid the rock on the ground and rubbed my hand. I noticed small flakes of mica covering my palm, mica that reflected sunlight in such a way that my whole hand seemed to be a magical wand as I waved it in front of me.

Christina opened her eyes and looked at me in her deadpan way.

"Money." That was all she said.

I stopped waving my hand around and leaned toward her.

"You are confusing me," I replied.

"On purpose. I want you to figure it out. Then you will better understand, and implement, what I am trying to teach you."

Of course I didn't get it right away. I had work to do—bills to pay, traditionally a difficult time for me. I kissed my cow on her pointed forehead and walked back to the house. I could hear her begin to chew cud as I closed the gate behind me.

Back inside I decided to face the unpleasant task. I stacked all the bills in front of me on the table, leaving the largest ones in the back. I couldn't bear to open them. With the economy in a slump, our income was simply not meeting our expenses, especially the mounting vet bills for my old dogs. I knew I could put those bills in the back of the pile for now, but I also knew that I would have to face them before the end of the day.

Up I got from the table to walk the familiar frantic circles around the living room, clenching my fists, chin to chest, eyes tearing up. I stopped pacing long enough to look out the window, bleary-eyed. A broad and familiar face stared back at me across the dogs' fence, eyes all but unblinking, locked to mine. Not even the mouth moved in punctuated cud-chewing. The silence between us was eerie and profound.

Okay. I heard the call. Once again I shuffled sadly out through the gate to stand before my fierce and determined teacher.

"You need me," Christina said quietly, no emotion in her steady voice.

The wind rasped at my throat, making my own words awkward and rough, reflective of my life. "In what way?" I responded.

"There is still no peace in your aura today. Have you forgotten the Heart exercise already?"

"It's just that the money thing is so all-powerful," I replied. "More expenses all the time, and not enough money to cover them—how are we humans supposed to manage?" Christina moved her feet as if practicing her line dancing. I thought I heard her whistle, but realized it was only the wind picking up in the still mostly bare tree limbs. She appeared to be ignoring my words and my great and overwhelming distress. As I turned back to the house, she looked up at me with those piercing eyes.

"There is always more than enough—of everything. In fact, there is no such thing as enough. Why even have a word in your language that limits? I shall say instead that there is always more-to-overflowing. Now, help yourself."

"Yeah, sure," I replied sarcastically. "How would you know about expenses and income and…" She stopped me short by raising her chin. When she once again lowered her head, she spoke with a hint of sorrow:

"Do you think I don't have utility bills and credit card payments, just like you? And my radio show business—nothing but expenses lately, with advertising revenue down. Just last week my accountant told me—" She stopped then, possibly because I was jumping up and down in front of her, frantically waving my arms.

"Whoa there—accountant?" I sat down abruptly. Following my lead, Christina bent her front legs at the knees and whumped to the ground beside me. Oddly, her warm breath was comforting. "I don't understand," I said glumly. Truthfully, I was having enough difficulty with the whole radio show idea without trying to understand why any cow would need an accountant. But then again, this was Christina talking.

"Nothing and no one on this planet is restricted to a what-you-see-is-all-you-get scenario. But, being human, your brain only wants to deal with what's right in front of your face, so to speak. I, however, being Cow, am aware of all possibilities because I listen to my Heart, not my brain."

But my brain was winning out, and I was feeling completely overwhelmed by life. For the second time that day, tears poured down my face. The inner peace I kept on seeking seemed so far beyond my reach.

"Not at all!" my bovine friend assured me. "It's not as hard as you think. My choice of realities is rather fun, actually, as well as peaceful."

"But you said you had financial problems, too."

"Oh," she said, waving her front hoof in the hay, "just an idea I like to play around with occasionally for amusement. No big deal."

"And do you have an IRS in that idea of yours?"

"Absolutely not!" she replied quickly. "Much too loaded a concept for even an enlightened cow as myself. I have, you see, learned over many lifetimes to choose my thoughts, situations, and acquaintances wisely."

"And have you also chosen me?"

"Yes," she said bowing her large head. "As your devoted friend and teacher, I can help you through the initial stages of conscious thought formation so that you, too, will eventually always choose wisely." She looked back up into my eyes. "And the truth is, I need you as much as you need me. You are such an excellent companion!

"Remember," Christina continued, in a whisper: "First, find your Heart center and create your peace. Then, release all your worry into that peace and allow the solution to find you. Give your concerns over to peace, and clarity will emerge. I promise."

Trusting her, I closed my eyes, mentally submerging my fears and woes in a beautiful pool of still, clear water, and I waited, allowing only the best to resurface. And then, ever so slowly, it came—the perfect answer for a once seemingly impossible problem. I smiled.

"Excellent," my beloved cow said kindly.

Returning to the house, I sat down at the table and with Heartfelt gratitude, mentally thanked the electric company for providing us with electricity; thanked the credit card company for allowing me to pay my veterinary bills promptly; sent blessings to everyone involved in farming, trucking, selling the food and other supplies I buy each week. Then I picked my best pen—my good-luck pen, I called it—to write with. It was covered in tiny shiny mirrors, and I was impressed by how much it reminded me of the mica-covered stone. The pen even felt rough-edged and prickly in my hand, but the light it gave off its surface always drew me back to using it.

As I wrote out the first check, I began to once again worry about finances. I found it hard to write the numbers I had to pay: painful, prickly, just like the stone when I closed my fist around it, and I emotionally drew away. As I stared into space, something caught my attention—the light, sparkling off the pen's many-faceted surface, bouncing around the room, careening off the mirrors. Intrigued, I turned it this way and that to create enchanting designs and colors. The light was brilliant but soft, easy to play with, easy to employ in a richness of joy I had not felt in some time.

Hmmm, the flashlight... *Grasp the flashlight firmly in one hand,* the instructions had said. *Step boldly forward with assurance...* * *Be sure the flashlight is turned on.* I let the light into my mind, invited it to brighten all those dusky regions filled with frightened thoughts. *Generously offer a hand-up to anyone behind you,* I remembered Christina reading to me. I thought about so many people working hard to help the animals, and now, more than anything—yes, boldly with assurance—I wanted to share what money we did have, with them, even if only in a small but consistent way. *By doing so, be assured this [flash]light will always provide all the direction in life you will ever need.*

Christina had stopped reading after that sentence, so I wondered what the instructions had said next. Immediately, words popped up into my mind like the old Magic Eight Ball: *Believe in Who You Are and go forward. Nothing more is required or needed to guide you.* And that was all it said.

Like gently laying the small rock back on her parent Earth, with a sense of honest peace, I paid all the bills. Then I sent donations to the animal sanctuaries, returning to the Whole of Life from my own supply without my usual attending fear of financial shortage. I found it all surprisingly easy. No prickly pain; only a deep feeling of appreciation and gratitude given from an unclenched fist. A memory of peace that, like my beautiful cow, was magnificent, ancient, dependable, and strong: my flashlight—my compass, and definitely a keeper.

25 OLDING

MID-APRIL: AT LAST, MY BIRTHDAY. I AM ALWAYS EXCITED ABOUT "MY DAY"—I love being on Earth, being alive, all the colors and sounds and textures and adventures and, uh-oh, can't ignore the increasing aches and pains and limitations of...

"Getting old," I grumbled to myself, despite my impending celebration, "is a nuisance." Afternoon shadows lay across the mountains; the wind picked up the chilly air; even the birds were more silent for the unexpected cold spell. And my knees hurt.

"I wouldn't know," a soft voice said from the depths of the center barn stall. "I look forward to my olding." A rumble and a burp identified the mystery voice as that of my exquisite bovine.

"You mean *aging*," I said.

"Well," Christina replied, shifting her weight amid her warm bed of hay, "you can 'age.' I intend to 'old.' I prefer that word—it has that comforting round sound of the 'O' that implies completeness and perfection, growing into balance with humility while ever evolving into something finer. In fact, I would say that *olding* means I am continually returning into my fullness, my inherent immortality."

"You're *immortal?*"

"Absolutely," Christina sighed, closing her eyes. I thought I heard snoring.

Let it go, I told myself. I wouldn't be at all surprised to learn my cow was ageless.

"Oh, the *body* will age," my sleepy cow said, "just as yours will."

"Thanks for reminding me," I said dismally. I rubbed my arthritic right hand.

"But we are not just our bodies, my friend," she continued. "Yes, they are our vehicle for a time. But who we always are in our true Selves was never born, will never die, and will never age. It is the aspect of yourself I have been helping you to find all these months. And even though I am rather enjoying being Cow, the ageless, boundless 'me' is the part of me I most choose to identify with. You can choose your ageless self as well. It's a personal choice everyone makes for themselves. Take it or leave it, it's the truth."

I guess I had sufficiently disturbed her nap that she now felt compelled to rise from her bed of hay and emerge to see what the rest of the neighborhood was up to. She poked her head around the stall's entrance and looked up at a robin high up in the fully leafed maple tree by the back door.

"If you remember from our previous lessons," she said, now enthusiastically in her lecture mode, "we're really pure energy, temporarily focused in a particular form—cow, human, that bird—including her song, the color of her feathers and her thoughts and dreams. Everything is one magnificent flow of energy." She turned to look directly at me with her most disciplined gaze. "Nothing—may I repeat, please— *nothing* is outside that stream of energy, nor does anything termed 'growing old' or 'dying' or otherwise, interrupt the flow of that energy. Energy is seamless, boundless and immortal, the fabric of Spirit that everywhere-everything-everyone, or to simplify: everything *is*."

I was lost, as usual. "Is *what?*"

Christina sighed, with just a tinge of impatience crinkling her ears into the forward position. She looked down her broad nose at me to say: "Everything/one is energy flowing in perfect order, in and out of physical time and space."

"Oh."

Christina brightened. "Did you say, 'O'?" She was obviously under the impression that I had gotten her point. The truth was, however, I continued to feel as if I was aging at an alarming rate, even though I still loved adventure and the exploration of inner levels of soul and mind. The body, however, is not always willing to follow. Actually, I thought it might be time for a nap. Christina, of course, read my thoughts. To demonstrate her next point, she shot out of the stall, bouncing about her field at top speed. Her long tail stood straight out behind her as she shouted aloft: "Be spontaneous!" This routine was then followed by snorting to a thundering (literally) of hooves supporting a very mortal body. "Your energy is as boundless as the cosmos!" she bellowed as she rounded out her third push about the field. She did seem a bit winded. Was that last lap just a tad slower? Did I see a slight limp in her immortal front leg? Sweat glistened on her back, despite the cool air. At last she came to a dead halt just short of completing a body slam into the barn wall. I distinctly heard her say, "Oops."

I, on the other hand, had been hunched over, trying to stay warm while nursing my chronic lower back pain and snuffling in anticipation of impending seasonal allergies.

"Preparing to suffer?" Christina asked between huffs. She squinted up those enormous brown eyes and dropped her eyelashes for emphasis. "It is your choice, you know."

"Quit making fun of me," I fussed, rubbing my left knee. "My aches and pains are real. I think *you* are just in denial. Ha!"

Christina sighed and turned her head down. Triumph was mine; could I actually be right for once? I sneezed repeatedly while hopping up and down on legs stiffening with the cold air.

"The trouble with humans," she began, raising those deep, piercing eyes to mine, "is that you all believe what the media tells you—and the politicians, the three thousand or so religions, the pharmaceutical companies—anyone who pretends they are smarter than you. They tell you that you are skin and bones, blood and tissue; that you are your job, your education, your age; but they never mention the most important thing. You see, you are so much more. Only you can know the truth for and about yourself. On the energetic level, no one is smarter or more authoritative or healthier than anyone else. That's true for humans, animals, trees, rocks, wind. If you have ten days, I'll give you the list. Everyone knows in their own soul who and what they truly, essentially are."

I took a wild guess. "Immortal?"

"Bingo. And whole. And without boundaries. You are simply a field of energy at play in the One field of energy. So, enjoy it, and get over your aging self."

"But my back and hand and knees and…"

Christina inched over until her nose was touching my shoulder. "What are all those pains telling you? What doors are they opening for you? How are they bringing you closer to who you really are?

What is the truth of Who You Are that they are trying to tell you? They are attention-getters, in all the best and most supportive, enlightening ways. Listen to them as wise teachers, not as your enemies."

But as much as I wanted to believe her, the longer I stood in the cold, damp air, the more I ached and the less patience I had. I felt unmistakably frail. Philosophy was failing me. My enormously rotund and sensible teacher, beautiful in her dense auburn-and-white coat and gentle ways, intuitively read my distress. She laid her chin across my shoulder and immediately, warmth flowed through me from my head to my feet, as if I were being bathed in a soft, heated waterfall. All feelings of physical distress and self-pity evaporated.

"When you start feeling aged," she said softly, "focus all your thoughts on being pure energy. See yourself as Old, in the best sense of the term. See yourself as dancing atoms and molecules *and the spaces between them*, just as vibrant and valid as the sun. Practice this often enough and you, too, will know your immortal self. And when, in natural time, the body falls away—as it must one day—you will simply step out as your sparkling, radiant self, and run free."

"Will you be there to meet me?" I asked.

"You can count on it," she said, leaning back and squaring her nearly nonexistent shoulders. "After all, I did choose to be here with you— because you need me, yes, but also because we are old friends." Her voice dropped to a whisper: "And I shall always be with you."

I stopped feeling sorry for myself.

"Oh, by the way," Christina said as she turned away, "Happy Birthday."

26 STICKING TO FLEXIBILITY

MID-MAY: A MAGNIFICENT VIRGINIA MORNING WITH SUMMER ALREADY clearly in an early lead, with abundantly blooming gardens, twice-mown lawns, and temperatures ballooning into the seventies. I stepped outside at 8:00 AM. and inhaled the sweet fragrance of early honeysuckle growing along the back fence, climbing up over the old hog shed, and winding through the branches of pines, shagbarks, and poplars. Christina was up according to her quite precise schedule, working her way toward the fence by the back door. While on this day there was no longer icy ground to slow her up, she did seem to be moving more deliberately than usual. And then I noticed she was limping. As I swung open the back gate leading from the dogs' garden, she came to a halt and twisted her head around to study her foot.

"Well, fancy that," she exclaimed, trying to lift her back right hoof forward. "There seems to be a bit of a stick poked in between my toes. Would you be so kind..."

Despite the birthday weight I had accumulated, I crunched my body in half to appraise the situation, ever eager to assist my bovine friend. Indeed, a smallish stick appeared to be wedged tightly between the mud-packed toes of my edgy cow.

"Quit *shifting*," I protested. Her swaying from side to side did present quite a challenge as I attempted to grab the barely visible offending bit of wood and pull it out. But it would not budge. Cow bulk drawn downward in Earth's gravitational field did nothing to ease the job. If we were to succeed here, she would have to lie down and extend her foot.

"But it's not time for me to lie down yet," she complained. "According to my schedule, first I eat breakfast, after which I am due to wander aimlessly to that dead tree down in the pasture and give my back a good scratch. Then I will forage for leaves and such, wander up the

151

fence line to the water bucket, have a long drink, stand in the sun for oh, a bit of time, *then* head back without pausing to the northern pasture position. There I will lie down and begin my late-morning nap. At such time and place I will be very happy to extend my foot. Any questions?"

"Only one," I said dryly. "Can you give just a little here?"

"No," she stated flatly. "Schedules are meant to be kept."

"Fine," I replied. "It's your foot, your stick."

"Sounds like the beginnings of a country music song," she said pensively. And she began to hum softly, swaying again to her own inner rhythm as we moved side-by-side toward the barn, where she worked her way through breakfast. Eventually, lyrics were forthcoming: "It's your stick and it's your foot; I'd help ya, honey, if I cout—"

"Don't you mean, *could?*" I interjected.

Glowering at me, she continued: "If I *cout*. Has to rhyme with *foot*." She stopped in mid-phrase and stared into space, the rest of the song obviously eluding her.

I thought I would help her out: "But you're as stubborn as a mule, *sticking* fast to your sch-e-*dule*."

"Lord only knows," she continued after me, picking up the beat, "a stick in the toes don't feel so good. Please help me, darlin', if you would." And she ended on a high note, head held high.

I applauded; she bowed.

"Thank you kindly," she said, turning on her heels and limping off. "Time to wander down to the tree now."

I watched her hobbling, obviously in pain, across the ground made bumpy by ambitiously burrowing moles. It would be at least an hour before she settled down once again. I turned back toward the gate. Time for my coffee; I couldn't be missing that. And then it would be close to noon, time for me to check my e-mail and work on accounts. After that, I would be taking the dogs out again to play, and I'd need to refill the water buckets. I liked my day to fit together neatly like a jigsaw puzzle.

A small cough interrupted my thoughts. I looked around to find a large, heavily breathing beast leaning slightly to the left, her right back foot lifted tentatively off the ground. "I don't suppose you could take that moment now," she said quietly. I thought about how my coffee time was fading away. So many things to do, so little time in which to do them. "I could lie down right now," she said with some effort. Obviously, changing her schedule was as painful for her as the stick caught between her toes. Or was it? I looked at her foot. The soft padding between her toes appeared somewhat red and swollen. "Sure," I said.

"But over here, on the northern side of the pasture, if you don't mind," Christina said, turning in that direction.

"But there's hay right here," I pointed out. "Easier on my knees, and for you, too."

"Perhaps," she said reluctantly, "but it's the place I'm supposed to be at..." She stopped mid-sentence, studying my face. "You don't get it, do you?" she said.

"Yes, I do," I replied. "It's a control issue, isn't it?"

She looked offended. "There's a stick in my foot, for goodness' sake! And it hurts. I'm trying to bend here, but I can't give in all the way."

"Well," I said, "I don't fancy walking all the way up-pasture when this spot will do fine. Did I mention this is my coffee time?"

I swear her lower lip quivered. Maybe she was feeling the morning coolness still lingering in the air. Or maybe she was genuinely concerned about my coffee break? More likely, she was feeling a loss of control over the situation. After all, it seemed to be a mere stick in the foot that was really calling the shots here. She turned and studied the distance between the barn and pasture. She turned back and studied my ain't-gonna-budge-on-this-one expression. And then she studied her foot. Between deep sighs Christina moaned. "How am I ever going to get my schedule back on track? But if I must..." Dramatically, she heaved her auburn self to the soft bed of hay at our respective feet and extended her right back hoof. With a swift and easy tug I pulled the stick from between her toes and the job was complete. Barely fifteen seconds had elapsed. I wondered how profoundly her schedule had been interrupted.

"So, off you go on your morning foraging," I said cheerily, moving back toward her head. But the odd thing was, she had gone to sleep, head tucked back, cheek against her neck, soft burblings emanating from her mouth. So, what of schedules, I guess, when the hay is deep and comfy and a friend is near? There was still time for my coffee, but what the heck—I settled down beside her to ponder the value of flexible schedules that invite new and unexpected twists and challenges to the day.

27   LIBERTY

WHEN CHRISTINA AWOKE FROM HER NAP AND NOTICED SHE WAS IN FRONT of the barn at the wrong time of day, at first she seemed confused and cranky. Her realization coincided with my own that I had missed my morning coffee, making me groggy and cross. We were quite the pair!

Christina shuffled to her feet while I brushed hay off my jeans. I finished cleaning her stall while she admired her stick-less hoof. Then we nodded to one another and moved in opposite directions, she toward the upper field and I toward the house. But at that moment, something strange occurred. Perhaps it was our mutual willingness to be "off schedule"; who knows what causes an obvious shift in energy fields, making human and cow turn back toward one another, *knowing* something unexpected is about to happen? Christina vigorously switched her tail back and forth, the bovine equivalent of delightful awareness, while for me, the whole universe suddenly appeared to be an enormous, miraculous, and mysterious place in which to live and play. This was not the inner peace or spiritual stability I had initially come seeking, but a much broader, deeper understanding of what it means to "belong"—to know my place within and *as part of* everything in range of my five physical senses, and beyond, way far beyond. Christina, reading my *satori*, or "aha!" moment of realization, was thrilled with the milestone I had reached, and, like the best teachers, rejoiced in my progress.

Apparently she was so thrilled that she felt I was ready to move forward in my learning, for she beckoned me to follow her as she walked to the center of her pasture and opened a door. No doubt about it: She took that left front hoof of hers and, raising it just so, shoved respect-fully at something visible only to her. Foot replaced on the ground, she watched that *something* swing away from her, and then she strode on through. Or, appeared to. It had to be a door. Couldn't have been a window, or she would have gotten stuck. Granted, it would be just like her to choose a window over a door. Yet, while nothing appeared evident to me, human deduction (limited though it may be) determined that what Christina had encountered, mastered, and moved past was not some insightful spiritual lesson, but simply a common door.

Well, un-common and un-doorish, for call me nearsighted—all I saw was grass and distant trees. *And where was she going?* Not far from the un-door was the real fence, and she was heading straight for it as if it were not there. And then it wasn't. And neither was she.

We've all heard about how cows get out, stand in the road, trample the garden—normal things one expects to deal with if one chooses to farm. But an evaporating cow was a great responsibility for me to bear. In despair and concern for her well-being, I slouched to the ground, feeling very much the victim. A slight hiccup behind me immediately pulled me back to the moment at hand. Or what the Buddhists so accurately say, to being *present*. A beloved and very solid russet-and-white creature stuck her broad chin over my shoulder as she sank down beside me.

"Did I miss anything?" she asked casually. With a yawn and a curl of her tail, she closed her eyes for her *usual* morning nap.

What to do. What to say. What to think. Such an all-encompassing beast, a profound enigma at the very least, and quite annoying. Christina could read my mind like a cheap novel, down to the nuances of hidden, silent judgments. I tried to focus on a piece of clover, to pay attention to all the detail it offered.

"Don't be silly," the sleepy cow said, not bothering to lift her long white lashes. "If you want to know, just ask. There are no secrets between us."

"No kidding!" I cried. "I can't have a single private thought without you invading."

"No harm meant," she replied evenly. "It's just that your thought forms are quite looming today—hard to miss, you might say. But you really haven't got a clear image of the door or the disappearing fence. I thought perhaps you would like an explanation."

"Yes, I would," I stated, as curiosity overpowered my pride. Immediately her left ear swiveled forward, then straight back as she slowly opened her eyes and looked fully at me. There was no judgment in her eyes, only kindness and great excitement.

"Good," she said. "It's all about liberty." she began. "Whatever in your heart you choose, you may have. Your *intention* is your choosing, and for you to find peace for yourself, you must choose from the truth that is yours and unique only to you. Then, what you do with what you choose remains an issue between you and your conscience. But you have to know, absolutely, that what you choose, you will—eventually—have. The complete realization of that choice will depend on the strength or weakness of your thoughts regarding it."

"And that has what to do with the door?"

"By way of example, this morning I chose to try something new," she replied. "It was more expedient to use the door than the escalator. I was visiting friends."

"You weren't gone long," I countered.

"Two weeks. We had a lot of catching up to do."

I looked for the watch I had forgotten to wear that morning. But did I expect to find weeks marked there?

Christina laughed. "Still stuck in illusion, are you? I thought we covered that in lesson 52A. This morning you chose to shovel manure (and, by the way, thank you for cleaning my stall), and I chose to visit friends, both very worthy endeavors. And to do so, we both chose doors. Yours connected your kitchen to the backyard, while mine connected to, let's just say, greener pastures. Same stuff, different players, all appropriate."

I studied Her Largeness, wondering how such a multi-pound beast could so easily move through invisible doors and dissolving fences. I would have asked aloud, but she was already studying something above my head. Those darn thought forms again.

"Liberty, again," she replied nonchalantly. "Poundage is within the mind, not the other way around. The Mind—yours, mine, the rooster's, everyone's—enfolds each of us in a unique way while simultaneously holding the overall Whole pattern of *Life*. Besides," she added brightly, "I'm pretty clever. I multitask, you know." There was that gleam in her eye that could set hay bales on fire.

"Could I go through that door?" I asked cautiously. Christina studied me thoughtfully, then answered with great care and kindness. "Perhaps another time, after a few more lessons, with a little less clutter in your mind," she said. "The key is focus and intention, and you have some practicing to do in both areas." I must have looked disappointed. In fact, I was relieved, not at all sure what might actually lie on the other side of some floating door.

"You've come a long way these last few months," she said softly. "With patience and practice, soon you will be able to achieve anything you choose. It's that simple. The very definition of liberty is the freedom to choose, to make your own way in a world of your own creation."

Yup; now I understood just how unready I was, since I could hardly figure out what she was talking about!

And now it was definitely time for that cup of coffee.

28   GETTING ACQUAINTED

CHRISTINA MEANDERED BACK UP TO THE NORTHERN END OF THE pasture, right on time for her late-morning nap, as if a two-week journey was just a blip in time. She folded down effortlessly onto the grass and rolled over on her side in the sun. It was one of those perfect days—not quite hot, with a sun as comforting as warm buttered toast and everything green and blooming. Patrick and Sito, the two resident goats, stretched out in their favorite dirt patch, swishing their tails to form plumes of dust, while nearby, a robin poked tentatively at the moist soil beneath the maple. What a day! Too lazy to deal with the pile of work on my desk, I strolled back outside, coffee in hand, to sit with my back up against Christina's shoulder. Her sweet smell—like Crayola crayons—flowed through my senses.

"Don't really know her that well," Christina said suddenly, without any preliminary explanation.

"Eh?" I asked sleepily.

"Jacquelyn, my friend in London. A lovely cow, Swiss Dairy, you know. She has her peculiarities, but she's a likable sort." I was not following her train of thought, but since she had now bent her head all the way around in order to look directly at me, I thought it only polite to participate, or at least, to *look* interested.

"There was that one instance," Christina continued, "when she gathered up this enormous pile of stones and placed a single acorn on the top. At the time I thought she needed help."

"Should I be following this?" I asked, beginning to feel disoriented. "But as it turned out, it was the acorn who needed help. *Jacquelyn* knew exactly what she was doing."

"All right, tell me about the acorn."

159

Christina, who had begun picking at her back hoof, swung her head up and around to look me square in the eye.

"Oh, I didn't know the acorn personally at all, because my friend said it had, you know, 'issues,' and that I should be very careful what I said around it. And one thing about Swiss Dairy cows, they know their acorns."

I took a deep breath. "And the pile of stones?"

"ENORMOUS!" Christina replied, rolling her eyes back and forth. "You would not believe the effort it must have taken to gather up—"

"Yes, yes," I said, hastily interrupting her. "It was a big pile of rock, I got that—"

"Stones—and plural, lots of them."

"What's the difference?"

Christina just looked at me. "Rock, my dear," she began in her lecture mode, "tends to be jagged and volcanic, determined, dense; a ponderous, often fiery, almost angry kind of soul. Stone, however, especially *stones*, are more profound, old, very wise and diplomatic souls, group-oriented, bonded by love and compassion. Usually sedimentary. *Such* a difference of character. I am surprised you haven't noticed."

To be honest, I hadn't given much thought to the difference between rock and stone; they were all *mineral* to my mind. I love stones/rocks, have always had an eye out for special ones, and often will carry a small one in my pocket. Once, I would swear one spoke to me.

Christina was studying me patiently while my brain reminisced. "Tell me about the stone who spoke to you," my benevolent cow said quietly. She shifted her bulk in the grass to settle into a more comfortable position. I knew by this move that she expected a full and detailed accounting.

"Well, it wasn't the same one that got caught in your foot, but it was really lovely," I said hesitantly. "I can't be sure it spoke to me, and why would it have spoken to me, anyway, because stones don't talk, and I was having a terrible day and..." I trailed off as Christina just looked at me with her unsettling deadpan expression.

"Tell me about the stone who spoke to you," she repeated, not shifting her eyes away. I knew then that I was in trouble. "No disclaimers, just the facts." And with that, she went silent. I took a very deep breath. Was she testing my sanity? I began anyway.

"I was having a terrible day..."

"You said that already."

"And my head hurt. I walked into the woods to find some peace. I sat down on a log and right there by my feet was a smallish rock—"

"Stone."

I stopped and stared at her.

She looked right back at me. "Just trying to get the facts," she said calmly.

"And right there by my feet was a smallish *stone*."

Christina leaned in toward me. "How do you know it was a stone and not a rock?" she asked. I thought for a moment I was going to leap at her, but I counted to three instead, and then resumed my story. "I didn't know, and I could have cared less if it was a rock or a stone. It was very pretty, kind of bluish and round and, well, soft. Not mushy-soft, like a tomato, but soft like a bar of soap."

"Smooth?"

"Yes."

"Hmmm." Christina seemed to be pondering on something terribly profound. "Definitely a stone."

"Whatever."

"Was it humming?" she suddenly asked, ignoring my comment.

"Excuse me?"

"Did you listen to it, put it to your ear, try singing to it to see if it would sing along with you? Did you speak to it or tell it how lovely it was?" My cow seemed to be getting quite worked up.

"No. And no. None of it. I looked at it, and then thought about my problems. I was actually more interested in the two squirrels playing in the trees above me."

"So you ignored the stone," Christina said flatly.

"Well, yes. And then, no."

"Why? What changed your mind?"

"I *thought* it said something to me."

"Such as?"

"I thought it said, 'Could you please move me just a bit to the right?'"

"Hmmm." That was it, the whole comment from such a brilliant cow.

Then she seemed to rally. "So, did you?"

"Did I what?"

"Move the stone to the right?"

"No." I thought for moment. "I guess that would have been the polite thing to do?"

"Indeed, yes," Christina replied.

"Actually," I said, continuing my story, "I went back to the house and forgot about the stone, at least until the next day. I woke up in the morning thinking about that voice I'd heard. Well, didn't really hear, but there it was in my mind, clear as anything. I thought maybe it was just the wind in the pines, or the squirrels running up and down the trees. It didn't make sense that it would be the stone/rock."

"Why?" my persistent cow asked.

"Well, it was a rock, for goodness' sake."

"Stone."

"Oh jeez. Okay, a stone."

"They have their own language, you know."

I looked at her. I weighed what I thought I knew about the mineral kingdom against the fact that Christina had never misled me.

"I did go back out that next morning to the log," I said very quietly.

"And?"

"And, darn it, I found the little *stone* and moved it a bit to the right."

Christina let out a substantial sigh of delight. "Thank you," she said, nodding her head vigorously. "But why did you change your mind?"

I considered my reasons for a moment or two. There had been several, but the most important one was very simple. "Because," I said firmly, "I do believe everything has some kind of consciousness, by virtue of being energy in motion. And if that little... stone had asked me to help it, I was going to do just that. And if I was just imagining that it had spoken to me, well, there was no harm done either way."

"Covering your bases, as they say," Christina muttered.

"That's about it," I replied stubbornly.

"Stones speak," she said firmly. "And they also sing. They are creative and wise and willing to share their knowledge and talents. Usually, one has to ask. They will not intrude."

"But that one—"

"*Sometimes,*" she continued, "if a stone feels a person is a helpful soul, they will initiate a conversation. Apparently, that little stone had something to tell you."

"So why didn't it just come out and tell me?" I asked. I was disappointed to think I had missed such an opportunity.

"Protocol, my dear," Christina said. "There is a process to getting acquainted that is rather sweet, if you ask me. And by going back and acknowledging that stone's request, you have honored the stone—and most important, all stones, and begun the process. So the next time a stone—or rock—speaks or sings to you, you will know to listen. You will not be disappointed by what you hear, I promise you."

"What now?" I asked.

"Ah yes," my favorite cow replied. "Everything will all unfold exactly as it should, as long as you are patient and yet persistent, a fine edge to walk, but possible with my help. Shall we start tomorrow?"

"More lessons?" I cried.

"Oh, more than you can ever imagine!" And she rolled back over on her side in the sun.

29   EXACTLY RIGHT

SHE WASN'T KIDDING, EITHER. I AM ALWAYS SURPRISED BY HOW QUICKLY ANY strides I make toward achieving inner peace, understanding, and stability are challenged by events so dramatic they shake me back to reconsideration of everything I thought was real. Just when I dare to say, "Oh yes, I think I really get it now!," inevitably, something enormous appears as if to confront me with: "Oh, you *thought* so, did you!"

Nearly a year's worth of questioning, hard lessons, and Christina's ever-present guiding ways had brought me to what I considered a broader, more-compassionate place of centered living, a clearer view of all aspects of being. More often now I could look upon my "enemies," real and imagined, with the same equanimity with which I viewed my dearest friends.

Then, in mid-June, a turkey truck turned over on Route 151, spilling hundreds of already frightened and injured birds across the highway. While I had not witnessed the accident itself, I came upon the sprawling wash of white feathers hours after the incident. Everything inside of me felt ill and desperate. There was no place far enough away I could run to, to avoid the pain I felt throughout my mind, body, and soul.

It was bad enough, in my opinion, that those terrible transport trucks were open on four sides to the wind, cages stacked one on top of the other, row after row on huge flatbed trucks. Route 151 is a main road between turkey and chicken farms east of the Blue Ridge, and the slaughterhouses and rendering plants in the Shenandoah Valley. For someone with a tender heart who had many a beloved hen-friend die in her arms over the years, the whole poultry-as-property mind-set always evokes a cry of anguish from me whenever I meet the poultry trucks in my travels.

Naturally, the minute I got home from seeing the feathers and knowing exactly what had happened earlier in the day, I rushed into Christina's barn, flung myself down beside her, and began to cry. Between sobs I described it all to her. She continued to chew cud throughout my raging, then slowly turned dark eyes toward my wet face as I trailed off with something extremely rude regarding poultry raisers, farmers, truckers, slaughterhouses, and processing plants. But she didn't say a word.

"So," I asked desperately, aiming for that emotional support I needed so badly, "how do I deal with *this one* in a peaceful way?"

"Kind of a rough bump for you, wasn't it?" she finally replied kindly, obviously aware of my despair.

"You might say so," I said bitterly. While I wanted the whole scenario to disappear, I simultaneously had to have something profound to wrap around it all so that I could put it into some kind of perspective other than "tragic."

"But it is tragic," Christina replied, edging gently into my thoughts. "Not quite as you imagine it to be, but tragic nonetheless."

I wanted to say, "Please explain. Please tell me there is a cosmic order to all of this, that the birds knew it was their time to leave, that rather than suffering, the turkeys knew the experience brought them insight and inner growth, that they really were not afraid..."

"Oh, they suffered," she answered quietly. "And, they felt great terror and physical pain. Many died, even more lived to be transported on to the Valley to the slaughterhouses. In no way was there anything easy and uplifting in that experience."

I looked at her in astonishment. Suddenly I felt isolated from anything beautiful and serene. Confusion hardly had room to creep into my exhausted mind, but it managed to seep around the blazing heat of anger now roiling inside me.

Christina shifted her ample self to a more comfortable position and resumed chewing her cud, her neck stretched forward just so, her eyes partially closed as if in bliss. I had no words, no patience, no peace. I realized just what a short distance I had come in achieving anything remotely akin to spiritual awareness. It was quite possible that I hadn't made any progress at all.

Christina bobbed her head slightly. "Oh, you've made more than you think," she said. "Your pain and anger simply mean you are paying attention and that you care deeply. Many so-called New Agers are very quick to explain away the suffering of others as if it were karmic payback, or divine growth. Quite the opposite. And far too many look the other way, feeling no concern at all."

By this time I was up and pacing, walking around and around the stall in circles, not unlike my old dogs who had had brain tumors. *Ironic,* I thought, *because my brain feels as if it is blowing apart.*

"Do you remember we once discussed Schweitzer's ethic of Reverence for Life?" she said softly. "Well, because of that ethic, he had trouble killing the bacteria, knowing that they, too, were living organisms. Yet as a medical doctor, if he did not kill the bacteria, he could not save his patients. Quite a dilemma for such a compassionate and dedicated man."

"So what did he do?"

"He prayed for forgiveness and killed the bacteria. But he was very aware that by doing so, he was still taking away the preciousness of life."

"And how do you know all of this?"

"I was his cat, remember? I would sit on his desk for hours while he worked late into the night, silently reminding him that listening to his soul's voice would always lead him in the right direction."

"And?"

"And he did listen, did follow, and did great things. I really miss him, you know?"

"Yes," I said. I was remembering my little gold hen Luna, as she lay dying in my arms. And there were Robyn and Stella, the speckled hens, and Miss Peach, among so many others. They were hardly turkeys, but poultry nonetheless.

"All the same exquisite work," Christina continued with her own line of thought. "Tending to the living, tending to the dying, tending to those rebirthing into new worlds and dimensions and states of being. And always making choices."

"Meaning?" I had stopped pacing and hunkered down right in front of her. "You have just been made aware of a severe and painful incident in which many fine beings of intelligence and sensitivity suffered a great deal. All those birds... *but*—now that you have reacted in a very normal, human way, what could you choose to do next?"

It took a while for my brain to relax and my Irish blood to stop cooking, but in time I was able to breathe slowly, in a measured manner, allowing my mind to clear. A single word came to mind: "Pray," I said.

"Exactly right," she said. "And what will you pray for?"

"For peace, for light, for clarity, for understanding," I replied.

"And all for what?" she pushed.

I paused and counted my breaths in even slower measure, searching deeply for the answer, struggling against my confusion.
"For the turkeys."

"Okay, good. But for what else that goes further, deeper, wider?"

I could feel stronger, surer energy moving up from my heart center into my mind. "For the direction life takes us all," I stated with confidence. "Through the fire, through the storms, through the raging waters... All the experiences that burn and drown us."

"And why?" my cow whispered.

"So we—I, and you, and the turkeys, and the driver of the truck and the slaughterhouse workers and the factory farmers—can emerge free of the distresses of life and know within ourselves compassion for all beings in the essence of Reverence for Life." I breathed out; I had no more energy to be angry or to fight anything, even what I deemed as an injustice. So, I just closed my eyes and prayed.

Christina rocked back in the hay and studied me. "I'm impressed," she said finally. "Believe it or not, you have come a lot further in your understanding than you think you have. If it makes it any easier, you can partially view all of this, down to the turkey truck, as a test in your deter-mination of who you truly are in your highest, purest Self. What matters the most to you? What kind of person do you want to be, and how do you want to present that person to the world? And congratulations; you did good, as the saying goes. You get an A-plus."

As I thought about all those birds, tears poured down my face again. Then I thought about Christina, my beloved teacher, and how far she had so patiently brought me in my quest for truth and stability, never giving up on her student.

"All of it really is important then, isn't it—the easy and the hard parts."

"Yup," she replied, returning to her cud.

And then she just closed her eyes and prayed.

30 SO FAR, SO VERY GOOD

SO HERE WE WERE, TWO SOULS IN THE HAY—A HUMAN AND HER cow—devoted friends sending our combined prayers out on the wind to all beings everywhere. And as the prayer in my heart and mind grew larger and less desperate, the words became fewer, until thoughts of turkeys and bumblebees, past friends and future adventures, all whirled in exquisite, interlacing circles throughout my mind, nothing appearing to be good or bad, found or lost, hopeful or hopeless. Was this actually peace?

It was still June, definitely summer once again: hot, humid, and buggy, sweat churning like white-water rapids down my face, and fly-groupies dotting Christina's back. In the trees locusts whirred and hummed incessantly as they shed their skins and the sun blasted through the damp air, searing everything it touched. Behind the barn, the donkeys played tag-and-chase, and Nori was "it." Patrick and Sito stretched out in their grassy field, eyes half-closed in contentment, while close to my left, the measured sound of large square jaws grinding grass into mush made me drowsy.

Spectacular. There was no other word for it; life brazenly ever-so-right-in-your-face, and it felt so incredibly good. Christina chewed cud while I thought of iced tea and the past year's rocky search to find myself. So much wisdom generously offered to me by my loving russet-and-white teacher. After stumbling so many times, yet righting myself more quickly each time, through Christina's guidance I now could reach deep within in my heart's center to find tranquility, so pure, so comfortable, I could never be the same frantic person I had been just twelve months before. That person was a stranger to me now.

"Do you feel, then," my cow asked, once again rummaging through my thoughts, "that you have discovered your True Nature—who *Rita* is?"

"Honestly? I must have. How else could I feel so peaceful now?"

"And what's the best part of that peace?"

Without hesitation I replied: "Knowing that it is always here inside me, still and clear and endless, and this is true for everybody, no matter who or what they are."

"Yes," my sleepy cow said. "It is the great connector of all life, the common denominator of all beings. And how do you tap into that still, clear center?" Gently, she laid her broad head on my shoulder.

I recalled so many of our lessons together. "By being who I am—not anyone else, just me?"

"Exactly. Don't try to be a tree, or a rabbit, or a cow, or the stars—you are a human being. Be the best human being you can possibly be, honoring yourself and all others in the most responsible way."

Her reference to being responsible reminded me of all my obligations: bills to be paid, cleaning the house, returning phone calls—an endlessly rushing river of Things Needing My Attention. I sighed, rose, and turned toward the house. I knew it was all just part of being human, yet...

Then just outside the barn door I saw a slight movement in Christina's water bucket and I stopped, sensing something was in trouble, and I was right. A very young bumblebee had fallen into the water and was frantically paddling to stay afloat. I reached down and lifted the insect up and out to safety in the sun, where it could dry its wings. It was so sweet—the first baby bumblebee I had ever seen. Relieved to have been able to save its life, I watched with delight as the tiny creature gathered its strength and flew away. I had acted from my intuition and it felt so good to do so, to know who I am, not needing to give excuses to anyone.

Christina was intently watching something across the road. Following her gaze, I saw a small herd of deer grazing way off in the tree line between field and forest before the land sweeps up into the mountains. Ballroom Mountain itself shimmered hazy and silver in the midday humidity, like a twelfth-century Chinese painting. Breathtaking! I turned back to speak to Christina, but now her eyes were closing; cud safely processed, a cycle completed. Everything in order, as it should be.

I dove deep into my Heart center to rebalance before barreling back into my day, much preferring to move forward from a place of peace and stability rather than confusion and regret. Yes, just making those choices...

"And what is the *other* best part of that peace and stability?" Christina asked, without ever opening her eyes.

"The other best part," I said happily, "is that it reminds me of the truth that we all are, despite outer appearances."

"And in a word, what would that be?" she asked.

"Love."

"Bravo," Christina replied. "I'm proud of you, you know. Now, go and do all those necessary human things. Bring order to your house, pay your bills, and make your phone calls, but do it all with joy and confidence." She shifted in the hay, but instead of going to sleep, she raised her nose into the air. "Well, look at that," she said furrowing her nonexistent brow. "I'm nearly late for my meditation. What was I thinking?" And with that, she rose gracefully to all four hooves and strode with purpose in her eyes to her beloved battered trash can in the adjacent field. With her head pressed ever so slightly just beneath the ragged rim, she gently rocked the can so softly that even the fly-groupies who had accompanied her seemed to nod off to sleep. I yawned. How fine to be still and silent for a change. Even the trees seemed to sigh. Then, as abruptly as she had declared it time for her meditation, she was done. Her head popped back up, eyes wide, ears forward, as the trash can fell to its side without complaint. "See you tomorrow," she said brightly, turning her head to give me her most serious expression. "A brief review of lesson 463B, I think, then on to learning about bi-particle travel. Hmmm... Bring boots and a lunch. And don't forget your inner calf."

And then Christina walked away, nose buttoned to the grass.

PHOTO BY MICHAEL REYNOLDS.

EPILOGUE

SEVERAL YEARS AGO *I* HAD A SERIES OF SEVEN STORM DREAMS. In each of the dreams enormous black clouds would be roiling up over the mountains to the west and bearing down on my small farm. I would run outside, frantically gathering my goats, donkeys and Christina into the safety of the barn before lightning or wind could descend on us. But in each dream the storm would turn at the last moment to evaporate and we would all be safe.

In one of the dreams, as the storm built behind us, a foal was being born in the barn. As I have never had horses, I was puzzled by this. But my mother, a deeply mystical person, was excited when I told her. The birth of a horse, she said, meant great spiritual awakening. She insisted the dreams came with messages and I should pay careful attention to them. Although *I* did not see any messages I took her word for it, as wise and knowledgeable as she was in such matters.

But the last of the storm dreams was far different than the preceding ones. This time the storm not only did not turn away or evaporate, but advanced much faster, the entire sky turning a sickly green and black—a tornado sky, I've been told. Rain, thunder and lightning pummeled the woods, fields, house and barn. I had no time to gather my large animals into safety and I was frightened for them to the point of feeling physically ill.

I clearly remember, in my dream, looking out the kitchen window and there in her usual resting position on the grass, front feet tucked under her, was Christina, her head not bowed against the elements, but level and slightly extended, chewing her cud as if it was the sunniest of days. Even now I can see her calm face, her eyes half closed as her jaws rotated in their precise rhythm. No concern, no worry, no fear. Just being, right there in the middle of such ferociousness. She was, in the midst of chaos, the epitome of inner peace.

And that was the end of the dream—message delivered—and received. What a gift.

Christina continues to teach me timeless, universal wisdom that is freely, readily available to anyone who asks to learn. She cannot, nor would she, do my work for me. What she does offer are the tools that will assist me in finding my own way, in my own time despite the "storms" that inevitably descend into my life. And those tools, among others, are compassion and generosity; stillness, serenity, and gentleness. She encourages me to listen to my heart, then speak and act with only love, truth and kindness— for myself and all others. In her eyes I see and know strength, steadiness, tolerance and respect.

Just a cow? Hardly!

ABOUT THE AUTHOR & COW

Rita Reynolds has a long-standing love and respect for everything in nature, nurtured from an early age by both her mother and her maternal grandmother. For over three decades she has tended to animals—from ducks to donkeys—at her small sanctuary in the Blue Ridge Mountains of Virginia. Currently, her animal family includes two goats, two donkeys, seventeen cats, five (mostly elderly) dogs, and, of course, Christina. Rita is married with two grown sons, Michael and Tim. She is the author of *Blessing the Bridge, What Animals Teach Us About Death, Dying, and Beyond* (NewSage Press, 2001) and editor and publisher of *laJoie,* a quarterly journal regarding reverence for all life. She welcomes correspondence and can be reached through email at veggiecowtoo@gmail.com or through her website www.blessingthebridge. com. Christina is still happily giving advice and enjoying the Reynolds' sanctuary.

Rita and Oliver.